22/4/18

C000182826

A–Z of

Ephesians 3:16-19
Colossians 1:9-12

Dear Oliver,

It has been so exciting to see your journey with Jesus unfold and see Him transform you from the inside out, and to be a small part of that. Baptism is only the beginning, the adventure just gets better!

I hope this book encourages and guides you, my friend wrote it + his desire was that it was really practical, because being an Apprentice of Jesus is just that - I hope it is helpful!.

Hugs and Radio 4 comedy,

Eve ☺ x

'Matthew's *A–Z of Discipleship* provides an easy-to-follow road map for someone starting out on their Christian journey, yet possesses a level of depth to challenge even the long-term disciple. Filled with insights from a man on his own personal journey, the reader is introduced to the wonderful person of Jesus Christ. Wisdom permeates the text, but none more so than the encouragement to read the Bible and pray every day. How helpful this book will be for those searching, those with questions and those starting out on the road to a life of faith . . . I will use Matthew's book in mentoring young believers.'

Iain Boyd, senior executive at an S&P 500 international corporation

'*A–Z of Discipleship* is an excellent resource for both new Christians and seekers alike. Each of the twenty-six chapters is precise, pithy and punchy, and provides a wonderful overview of what it means to be a follower of Jesus Christ. Matthew Porter has done a great service in producing this informative and accessible resource and I heartily commend it.'

Greg Downes, Theologian and Missioner, The Belfrey, York

'This book is a prayer answered, the definitive post-Alpha-course, must-have read. A straight-talking, practical guide to following Jesus and exploring the liberating joy and freedom that discipleship brings. Like the gospel, this book is refreshingly simple, and a satnav to Christ.'

Warren 'Ace' Furman, evangelist and TV gladiator

'Don't be fooled by the size of this little book – it's powerful stuff! As Matthew says in his introduction, it might be best read in a few minutes each day over a month. But the themes are so rich that you'll find the words running around your mind throughout the rest of the day.'

Paul Harcourt, National Leader, New Wine England

'A book for anybody, whether new or mature in the Christian life, who seeks a deeper and richer faith. It overflows with virtues: realistic and scriptural, accessible and profound, compassionate and challenging. Read this book slowly over a month and let the effects bless the rest of your life.'

Revd Canon J.John, evangelist, minister, speaker, social activist and writer

'Matthew has written a supremely accessible guide to the Christian life for those wanting to follow Jesus.'

Nadine Parkinson, Network Relationship Manager, Tearfund UK

'I am delighted that my brother Matthew has distilled the wisdom of his many years of church leadership into this book on basic discipleship. Full of Bible insights, personal illustrations and practical advice, it should be a helpful resource for those entering into the journey of following Jesus. As my wife and I network across houses of prayer and prayer networks in the UK, we are aware that God is on the move in fresh ways. We are anticipating that there will be many thousands of new young Christians who will need a book like this to help them get good foundations of faith. I warmly endorse Matthew's writing.'

Revd Dr William Porter, Beacon House of Prayer, Stoke on Trent

'Discipleship is not an end in itself – it is the adventure of finding God's purpose in our lives and living it out, as we seek to follow Jesus in the power of the Spirit, to the glory of God the Father. Whether you have been on this journey for a while, or you have just begun, reading this book will help you grow in your relationship with God, in your service and witness to others, and in your participation in the life of your local church. Full of practical, biblical wisdom, it's a great book either to read at a stretch or to dip into each day. Remember, too, that to be a disciple also involves discipline where our thoughts and feelings, which result in our actions, are ruled by the Holy Spirit.'

The Rt Revd John Sentamu,
Archbishop of York

'Matthew is an accomplished church leader, a lifelong disciple and profound writer. He lives what he writes. I know because I have seen it year in and year out for over twenty years. He is the kind of person you would want and trust to write a book like this.'

Ric Thorpe, Bishop of Islington

'As a lifelong follower of Jesus, I found this book tremendously helpful. Matthew has taken the key components of our faith and created a wise, pastoral and deeply usable guide. It is designed for new followers of Jesus but rich enough in content that I learned and gleaned from it myself. I am thankful to know Matthew personally and witness the way he lives out his faith. As a church and ministry leader, I look forward to using this book as I invite friends to follow the God we love.'

Sarah Yardley, Festival Coordinator,
Creation Fest

A–Z of Discipleship

Matthew Porter

Authentic

First published 2017 by Authentic Media Limited,
PO Box 6326, Bletchley, Milton Keynes, MK1 9GG.
authenticmedia.co.uk

British Library Cataloguing in Publication Data
A catalogue record for this book is available from the British Library.
ISBN: 978-1-78078-456-4
978-1-78078-457-1 (e-book)

Cover design by Luke Porter luke-porter.co.uk
Printed in the UK by CPI Group (UK) Ltd., Croydon, CR0 4YY

Contents

Contents

Foreword

Discipleship is one of the most profound activities a human being can choose because it is a determination to live differently, to live not for oneself, but for someone else. That life is one of following Jesus in every area, with everyone, all the time. It is not exclusive to the holiest of saints but is for every person who decides to follow Jesus. It is simple, and yet profound; accessible to the youngest believer, and yet a lifelong journey of depth and transformation. It is one of the keys to living life well.

And that is why I am so grateful to Matthew for writing this book. Matthew has given us a book that helps start the journey, and accompanies us along the way. It is a book that is for today's church. It doesn't assume prior knowledge and, at the same time, doesn't patronize the reader who has some understanding already. It is laced generously with biblical references that can be followed up later or enjoyed at a slower pace. I loved the breadth of drawing on other sources and writers and speakers too. As I read it, I found I got a feel for the big picture, as well as finding the depth when I dwelt in a particular theme. As such, it is an ideal follow-up to the Alpha course, or other introductions to the Christian faith, and very useful for helping others to grow in their faith.

Foreword

As for the man behind the words, it is no surprise that Matthew has written this book. He is an accomplished church leader, a lifelong disciple and profound writer. I have known him since we were at college together in 1993 and we have met and prayed regularly together several times each year since then. Matthew lives what he writes. I know because I have seen it year in and year out. Throughout this time, he has always been the thoughtful one, always consistent, always dependable. Personal stories come through in every chapter. He is the kind of person you would want and trust to write a book like this.

And it is no surprise either to see a book like this come from the church Matthew is leading. The Belfrey in York has deep roots in encouraging discipleship. David Watson, who wrote a book with a similar name, was a previous vicar. This church has discipleship as part of its DNA. And yet this book is different from Watson's version. This one is written for to-day's missional context where new Christians are more likely to have no understanding of the Christian faith at all. It feels accessible too – something that is not a scary book for seriously committed saints but easy to pick up, easy to read and ab-sorb, and yet drawing the reader into a journey that will last a lifetime.

So let me encourage you (see chapter E!) to go on the journey using this *A–Z of Discipleship*. It will help you to deepen your relationship with God – Father, Son and Holy Spirit – and give you a solid foundation for following Jesus every step you take.

Ric Thorpe
Bishop of Islington

Preface

It was the birthday of my third son, Luke – 3 March 2013. I recall waking early, having had one of those dreams that stirs the heart and won't go away. In the dream I saw a book that I had authored. While I didn't see any of its chapter headings, I recognized that there were twenty-six chapters and they were all fairly short, simple and compact. It was a book for those who want to grow in discipleship. It had no long theological words and didn't assume any prior background knowledge. It was called the *A–Z of Discipleship*. This is that book.

I waited over three years to begin writing, partly because finding the time was not easy. We've been going through many changes at The Belfrey – the church in York that I'm honoured to lead – and leading my church has rightly dominated my time. But the delay was also because I wanted to cover the writing of this book in much prayer and make sure that it wasn't rushed and the timing was right. I also needed space to write and didn't find that until the summer of 2016 when I had a three-month period of sabbatical leave. I'm grateful to the Diocese of York and to the people of The Belfrey for that time. It was a time of profound rest, regeneration and experiencing the beauty of the wonderful world our good Father has made. Out of that rest I wrote this *A–Z*.

Much of the book was written at Bethel Church in Redding, California, in the context of worship, teaching, sunshine, and the kind hospitality of a church family committed to pursuing God's kingdom here on earth as it is in heaven. Some chapters were written in their prayer chapel as people around me rested in God's presence – some sitting, others standing or kneeling or lying on the floor. It was completed back home in York and I'm grateful to colleagues in York, especially Greg Downes and Ben Doolan, for their helpful comments and constructive feedback.

Because it originated in a dream, in many ways writing this book has been an act of obedience. Whether it sells well isn't my main motivation. Of course every author wants their book to be read – and I, along with my publishers, Authentic Media, hope that's the case and that this book is just the kind of thing that someone beginning to follow Jesus needs in order to help establish strong foundations for a life of discipleship. Rooted in Scripture and earthed in the life of a local church in one of the more unchurched regions of the world, it doesn't assume that being a disciple is an easy life. But it is a great life! The best life! My hope is that the Spirit of God uses this *A–Z of Discipleship* to help many capture a vision for a lifetime of discipleship that's not only personally fulfilling but, more importantly, changes the world.

Matthew Porter
St Michael le Belfrey, York
Easter 2017

Acknowledgements

I want to give special thanks to my wife, Sam, who has faithfully walked the journey of discipleship with me since we met in 1987. I could ask for no finer friend, wonderful wife or caring companion. To my sons, who are themselves beginning this great adventure of following Jesus. Keep going – it's the best life! To my father, Richard Porter, who constantly pointed me to Christ and now is experiencing God's kingdom fully in heaven. And to my mother, a faithful woman of prayer and the kindest person I know.

Introduction

This *A–Z of Discipleship* is a short, simple, no-nonsense guide to discipleship.

Discipleship is the daily practice of following Jesus. Discipleship is an exciting journey to which all Christians are called. Discipleship is an adventure. It's a lifelong experience of going where Jesus goes, doing what Jesus does and saying what Jesus says. David Watson says in his classic book, *Discipleship*: 'in calling people to follow him . . . [Jesus] called them primarily to him and not just to his teaching.'[1] That's why this book's central character is a person – the person of Jesus Christ.

There are many books available today to help us live life better, and most of them start with us. But the Bible, which is the handbook for discipleship, is different. As Rick Warren helpfully says in his opening words of *The Purpose Driven Life*: 'It's not about you.'[2] Disciples are those who've discovered it's all about Jesus.

Many are searching for identity, asking 'Who am I?' Many are searching for purpose, asking 'What should I be doing?' Many are searching for hope, asking 'What's my future going to be like?' For the last two thousand years disciples have found these questions and many others answered in the person of Jesus Christ.[3] He affects all understanding, imagining, living and breathing. The life of discipleship is all about Jesus. It starts with him and stands and falls on his life, death, resurrection and ascension.[4]

John's gospel – his good-news account in the Bible – starts with Jesus, saying: 'In the beginning was the Word [that is, Jesus], and the Word was with God, and the Word was God.'[5] This Jesus, present at the beginning, then came to earth two thousand years ago as God in human flesh to show us what God is like.[6] Our ancestors felt this was so significant for the history of humanity that they even re-dated time, centred around his birth.[7]

If you were to imagine God coming to earth and doing God-like things, what kind of things would he do? For most of us he would do things like love the loveless, forgive the sinner, give dignity to the broken, heal the sick and care for the poor. That's exactly what Jesus did. And more. That's why Jesus Christ is 'the image of the invisible God'.[8] He shows us God.[9] He shows us our need of God, and through his death and resurrection he's opened the way to a living relationship in the power of the Holy Spirit with the God he calls 'Father'.[10] This is the heart of the good news – what the Bible calls 'the gospel'. 'This gospel,' says the Archbishop of York, John Sentamu, 'offers forgiveness for the past, new life for the present, and hope for the future.'[11] In response Christ calls us to connect with him, to build our lives around him and to serve him.[12] This is what it means to follow him.[13] To live in relationship with him. It's the life of discipleship. And it all begins with the person of Jesus.

If you're not yet a follower of Jesus, this book will encourage you to make a start. It'll especially help you if you're just beginning the journey of following Christ. It'll also be useful if you've been a disciple for a while, enabling you to brush up on the basics and strengthen your foundations.

This book contains endnotes which are almost all Bible verses. In fact there are over 650 Bible references (with a few used more than once) in this short book. You can follow up each one and see how the Bible really does speak into contemporary life and help us live as disciples today. While I hope this *A–Z* is practical and helpful, don't forget that it's *the Bible* that's the main textbook for discipleship, not this book. In the end, there's no substitute for going to the main text. It might help to think of this *A–Z* as like reading a guide to a Shakespearian play. Those kinds of guides are useful summaries, but there's nothing better than reading Shakespeare himself. Similarly, my hope is that this book will inspire you to read the Bible for yourself and discover the wonder of Christ and the joy of following him.

It won't take you very long to read this book all in one go. However, if you want to get the most out of it I'd urge you to read it slowly, taking a chapter each day, giving time to work on the short 'Action and Prayer' sections at the end of each chapter and to write your reflections down. First thing in the morning would be best, enabling you to chew over and then put into practice the chapter's theme as you go through your day. Reading the *A–Z of Discipleship* in this way will take you just under a month.

My prayer for you as you read this book is that you will find it one of the most impactful months of your life, and that the Holy Spirit will draw close to you, speak to you and bring you lasting transformation.

Matthew Porter can be contacted at matthew.porter@belfrey.org

A is for Abba

Abba is one of the first sounds an infant makes as he or she learns to speak. It means 'Father'.[1] Similarly, learning to call God 'Father' is one of the very first things to discover on the journey of discipleship. That's why **A is for Abba**.

Many people start exploring matters of faith not knowing if God exists or, if he does, what kind of God he is. My friend Kevin was like that. He found himself intrigued to know more, after he saw the positive change in his wife when she began following Jesus. Soon he found himself talking to God saying 'If you're real, show yourself to me.' That began a journey which resulted some months later in me baptizing him 'in the name of *the Father*, the Son and the Holy Spirit'. Kevin is continuing to grow as a disciple today and is increasingly discovering that God the Father is good, trustworthy and deserving of all praise.

The Bible describes God as Father.[2] It doesn't say he is *like* a father, but that he *is* Father.[3] Jesus called him '*Abba*, Father'[4] and told his disciples to pray to him as 'Our Father'.[5] Jesus also said that God is a 'good' Father.[6] That doesn't mean God is human or male, because God is neither; he is 'spirit'.[7] Jesus simply means God is good and fathers us perfectly. Consequently I've discovered that if I want to father my children well, or be a good father to the people entrusted to my care, there's no better example to follow than the God and Father of our Lord Jesus Christ.[8]

Our good Father is the Creator. He's made a beautiful world reflecting his goodness.[9] In the same way that people want to know about the artist who painted an exquisite painting, or the architect who designed an inspiring building, so many are stirred by a magnificent sunset or a glorious garden and find themselves seeking after and worshipping the One who made our wonderful world.[10]

Humanity is the pinnacle of his creation, with God describing us as 'very good'.[11] He made men and women 'in his own image',[12] which means that together we reflect something of the nature of God and of his characteristics. The Father made us to love him and to live in relationship with him.[13] This has always been his intention, so why is the world imperfect? The Bible answers this question in its opening pages, saying that life is fundamentally compromised by human selfishness – what the Bible calls 'sin'.[14] Sin is wrongdoing.[15] Sin is bad. It goes against everything a good God desires, spoiling our world and all our relationships. At its heart, sin fractures our relationship with our good Father – so much so that, for many people, God feels distant or non-existent.[16] But the Bible tells the story of how the good Father, rather than rejecting us, has gone to great lengths to restore our relationship with him. He did this by sending his only Son, Jesus, to die for our sins and rise to give us new life.[17] Such is the love of the Father.[18]

As we put our faith in Christ, whose sacrificial death and resurrection have liberated us (see **J is for Jesus**), so we become 'adopted' into God's family, becoming his children.[19] This means that disciples have access to God.[20] They can live without fear or shame. They can encounter the presence of his Spirit (see **H is for Holy Spirit**). Know his love. Hear his voice.

Speak his word. Disciples are to reflect the family likeness and represent Christ to a hurting world.[21]

As sons and daughters of the good Father, we also inherit all the good things of God's kingdom that Jesus won for us when he died (see **K is for Kingdom**), experiencing them partly now and fully in heaven.[22] Our status changes (see **I is for Identity**) and we become what the Bible calls 'co-heirs with Christ'.[23] What an honour!

As we get to know Jesus, so we get to know his Father. In fact Jesus said that anyone who's seen him has seen the Father.[24] Some who've had a bad relationship with their human father can find it initially hard to relate to God as Father. If that's you, don't worry; just start to talk with him and allow what the Bible says about God the Father to shape you, rather than any negative experience of a human father.

Because God is a good Father he will sometimes allow us to go through experiences that will discipline us. This is not to vindictively punish us but rather to mature us, so we're more fit for purpose. All good human fathers do this if they love their children, and God the Father is no different.[25]

When people become Christians at The Belfrey in York where I'm vicar, they sometimes describe it as 'coming home'. There's a sense that they've been away and now they've returned and found a family in which to belong and settle. I like that. God the Father has a household and family in which we're to belong, and until that home is found there's an unsettledness deep inside.

We've recently welcomed into our family a teenage unaccompanied refugee who's travelled thousands of miles from a different country and continent, looking for a new home. As he's settling into our family we're praying that he finds a house-hold where he's safe to grow and flourish. As with my own children, I want to be – as best as I can be – a good father to him and I want him to know he's loved and that he can feel settled and secure. On a much deeper level our good Father knows that each of us is on a journey seeking faith and under-standing, and he wants to provide a home for our hearts. The fourth-century theologian Augustine expressed this beautifully in one of his prayers: 'O God, our hearts are restless until they find rest in you.'

For the last two thousand years women and men have found the rest that our Father longs to give, as they've begun to follow his Son, Jesus Christ. This normally begins by praying and tell-ing God that you want to follow Jesus. It's as simple as that! If you've never done that, why not begin talking with him? Start a conversation. Your good Father is present, and he hears and will reveal himself to all who come with an open heart.[26] Begin to read the Bible too (see **B is for Bible**), starting with one of the gospel accounts of the life of Jesus, asking God's Spirit to guide you and speak with you about this new life, lived in rela-tionship with your Father God.[27]

There's a really helpful course which explores what it means to be a disciple, called Alpha.[28] Thousands of churches across the world, including the church I lead – The Belfrey, use Alpha as a means of helping people begin the life of discipleship. If you've never done an Alpha course, I'd thoroughly recom-mend it.

At the heart of the story of God in the Bible is a good Father who sent Jesus Christ to enable each one of us to have a re-lationship with him by the Holy Spirit. This is the God who made you, loves you and is your Abba Father.

ACTION: If God really is a good Heavenly Father, do you want to know him and receive all the benefits of being in his family? Write down your honest reflections about all this. God has been present throughout your life – even at times when you didn't recognize his presence. Now look back on your life and consider and list some of the main ways that God has been looking after you, as your good Father. Then look up some of the Bible references for today. What stands out for you about God the Father? Write down your thoughts.

PRAYER: Read back what you've just written down and turn it into a prayer, telling God about it. He is listening and hears. If you're not yet a disciple, you could begin to follow today by simply starting to pray. You might like to pray this prayer:

'Father God, thank you that you're good, that you made me to love me and that Jesus died for me. I'm sorry for the many times I've been selfish and ignored you. As I begin to follow you today, fill me with your love, show me how amazing Jesus is and give me your Spirit to help me to follow you day by day.'

If you're already a disciple, tell Abba Father that you want to know him more fully and follow Christ more closely in these coming days. You might like to turn those thoughts into a written prayer. Write it down, so you can return to it in the coming days.

B is for Bible

Of all the books in the world, one shapes disciples more than any other: the Bible. Abraham Lincoln, renowned President of the United States through the American Civil War, said that the Bible 'is the best book that God has given to man'. John Wesley, founder of the Methodist movement, was well read and yet said of the Bible: 'Oh, give me that Book! At any price give me the Book of God. Let me be a man of one book.' When Elizabeth II was crowned Queen of England in 1953 she was handed a Bible by the Moderator of the Church of Scotland with the words: 'Receive this book, the most precious gift this world affords.' Disciples take the Bible really seriously! That's why **B is for Bible**.

The Bible is one book made up of two main sections – the 39 books of the Old Testament (which is basically the Jewish Bible) and the 27 books of the New Testament (making up 66 books in all). It includes history, prophetic writings, poetry, narrative, letters, wisdom and apocalyptic[1] literature. It proclaims the story of God's love and how our Heavenly Father desires relationship with people. The Old Testament begins with creation, telling how sin (wrongdoing) entered the world and explaining the story of Israel becoming God's chosen people. The New Testament describes the kingdom of God (see **K is for Kingdom**) and the life of Jesus Christ, and how through his death and resurrection humanity is saved from sin and its consequences, and includes the story of the earliest church and letters to encourage disciples. Followers of Jesus believe that the Bible is God's word[2] – his message – and that it's 'a lamp for my feet, a light on my path',[3] which means it helps disciples navigate well the path of life.

The Holy Spirit guides us and shows us the way ahead, as we read the Bible and do what it says.[4] The Bible is foundational to the life of the disciple. It's inspired and God-breathed, thoroughly practical and useful,[5] and as such it is Scripture (holy writing).[6] It is God's word.[7] John Stott, respected church leader of the twentieth century, used to say that the follower of Jesus should live with the Bible in one hand and a newspaper in the other. He recognized that we need the Bible to guide us in God's truth and the newspaper to root us in the contemporary world.

My mother's father – Wilfred Brown – was a disciple who prioritized the Bible. After beginning working life as a coal miner in a South Yorkshire colliery, Grandpa became quite successful in insurance. When he awoke each morning he'd normally find that the postman had been early and delivered the mail. He would come downstairs in the morning, pick up the post, go into his office and put the mail to one side on his desk. Then he would open his Bible and read. He would then pray, picking up some of the words of the Bible he'd read. He would dedicate his day to God, praying for his family and other matters on his heart. Having done these things, Grandpa would then open his post. I remember him telling me why he did things in this order; he said this: 'I want the first thing I hear every day to be the words of God, rather than the words of people.' I've never forgotten that and since then I've aimed to do the same. Rather than switch on social media or even hear the news, I prefer first to read the Bible. This prepares me for the day ahead. I urge disciples to do the same.

If you're new to the Bible, the best place to start is in the New Testament with one of the four gospels – Matthew, Mark, Luke and John – the four books that describe the life of Jesus. Get to know this person of Jesus. After this, dip into some of the rest of the New Testament and into the Old Testament too. As you read, ask the Holy Spirit to speak to you. He will. Learn to be attentive to his voice. Don't rush. You'll find that things begin to stand out and get your attention. Often this seemingly old book will speak into your situation with a surprising relevance, and you'll begin to hear God's voice in the Bible. You'll discover that what the Bible says of itself is true – that it is the word of God.

The Bible is quite a large book and can seem a bit daunting to a new disciple. Don't let its size put you off. If you read about ten minutes or so of the Bible every day, you'll have read it all in about a year. There are all sorts of reading plans you can find that help you to read it. The most important thing is to read it, every day. Allow the truth of God's word to begin to mould your life.

While there are some things in the Bible that are hard to understand,[8] most things are pretty plain and clear.[9] Don't forget that disciples of Jesus read the Old Testament with 'New Testament spectacles'.

Jesus came to fulfil the commands and laws of the Old Testament,[10] which means that while they're interesting and helpful to read, disciples of Jesus no longer follow them as Jews do.[11] There are books available that help disciples learn to understand the Bible and these can be really helpful. However, disciples need to take care, as it's easy to conveniently discard the bits of the Bible you find uncomfortable or twist the Bible to say what you want it to say. Don't do this! Rather, come under the Bible's authority. Preacher and author Leonard Ravenhill helpfully said that the Bible is not primarily to be explained; rather 'first and foremost it is a book to be believed and after that to be obeyed'[12] (see **O is for Obedience**).

There are all sorts of interpretative tools disciples can use to help us when we come across difficult parts of the Bible (that are beyond the remit of this simple *A–Z*). For our purposes it's important to realize that every text has a context, and understanding that context helps us on the few occasions when, on first reading, the Bible might seem to be inconsistent.[13] Very infrequently the Bible speaks with two voices on a bigger matter. The role of women in leadership has, in recent years, become a case in point. A good rule of thumb here is this: when the Bible is consistently clear on a matter, so should we be; when the Bible offers a variety of approaches, so can we.[14]

Disciples believe that the Bible is a living book.[15] While it mustn't be added to,[16] God still speaks and works and transforms through it. It's a disciple's key resource for life and prayer. It reveals God's will, and so phrases and sections can be helpfully used in worship and prayer as we pray that God's will would be fulfilled on earth as in heaven.[17] However, the Bible is not God himself. It is to be honoured but not worshipped. As Bill Johnson helpfully says: 'Remember, God is bigger than His book. The Bible does not contain God, it reveals Him.'[18] That's why disciples should always pray that through the written word – the Bible – humanity would come to know and experience the Living Word – who is Jesus Christ.

ACTION: Read 2 Timothy 3:16 and write down what the Bible says of itself. Then write how you're discovering these things to be true about the Bible. Are you reading the Bible every day? Resolve to do so. If you don't know where to start, begin with one of the gospels (e.g. Mark) and ask the Holy Spirit to speak to you as you read. Write down your thoughts and reflections as you read.

PRAYER: Look at the things you've written down today and thank God for what you're learning about him through his word, the Bible. Pray that the truth of his word would sink deep into your heart and increasingly shape your thinking, spilling out into action. Pray for an opportunity today to share what you're discovering about the Bible with a friend or someone at work.

C is for Church

Loneliness is pandemic in contemporary society. In all age-groups. From young people to senior citizens, we're all seeking friendship, connection and love – but many are failing to find it. Our Heavenly Father understands this longing, saying that we're not meant to live alone[1] but rather we're made for relationship. In his Great Commandment Jesus agrees, telling his followers to focus their efforts on two key relationships: loving God and loving people.[2]

Being a disciple is a great life. It's a fulfilling life. But loving God and loving people is challenging and not always easy, so it's good to know that nobody is invited to be a disciple on their own. Discipleship is not meant to happen in isolation. Instead we're called to follow Christ together with others, in community.[3] His community is called 'the church', which is why **C is for Church**.

In the Bible, 'church' isn't about a building or institution. It's about people.[4] It's a fellowship of Christ-followers. Nicky Gumbel, church leader and pioneer of the Alpha course, helpfully expresses it like this: 'Church is not an organisation you join; it is a family where you belong, a home where you are loved and a hospital where you find healing.'[5]

The church sometimes has a bad name. It's often criticized in contemporary media, and sometimes followers of Jesus can be made to feel embarrassed about being associated with church.

But Jesus died for the church – that's how much he values his people! When Colossians 1 lists some of the qualities of Jesus, it says incredible things – like Jesus is 'the image of the invisible God' and creator;[6] yet in the same list it also calls him 'the *head* of . . . the church'.[7] That's one of Christ's precious titles and shows how important 'church' is to him. Elsewhere the Bible calls the church 'the *bride* of Christ'[8] – his beloved. If Jesus is so passionate about his church – so much so that he's proud to head it up and be betrothed to it – so it should be important to his followers.

The very first church was birthed in Jerusalem just after Jesus' resurrection and ascension. You can read all about it in Acts 2. It began with three thousand people who decided to follow Jesus, were filled with God's empowering presence (see **H is for Holy Spirit**), and marked their commitment by being baptized. Led by the apostles,[9] the life of this new church is wonderfully described in Acts 2:42–47:

> They devoted themselves to the apostles' teaching and to fellowship, to the breaking of bread and to prayer. Everyone was filled with awe at the many wonders and signs performed by the apostles. All the believers were together and had everything in common. They sold property and possessions to give to anyone who had need. Every day they continued to meet together in the temple courts. They broke bread in their homes and ate together with glad and sincere hearts, praising God and enjoying the favour of all the people. And the Lord added to their number daily those who were being saved.

This was a hungry church. Hungry to be taught. Hungry to pray. Hungry to grow. And hungry to share life together in community. They did this in a larger setting ('in the temple courts') and in smaller gatherings ('in their homes'). I've found over the years that both the larger and smaller church gatherings are crucial for discipleship. The larger congregation is helpful for worship and celebration and for receiving inspiring teaching. But a smaller group that meets in a home is also important for supportive friendships, accountability and mission. For the last thirty years I've found that these two sizes of church gathering – the congregation and the group – have sustained and supported me as a disciple. Through them I've been able to give and receive. That's why I urge all disciples to join a church with congregations and groups. It's healthy and biblical.

We also see from Acts 2 that the earliest church was a community where miracles were normal and where people held lightly to their possessions. They expected God to be powerfully at work, trusted his provision and honoured their church leaders. They were happy and full of praise. All this resulted in two things. First, those who weren't believers treated them with respect – probably because they saw a quality to their lives and relationships which was authentic and good. We could do with more of this in our day. Second, the church kept growing. In fact every day people chose to follow Jesus! God still wants this for the church today – even in places like Europe and the UK where many people associate church with decline rather than growth. David Watson knew this to be true, which is why, arriving in York in the 1960s to lead a declining church, he famously said: 'If anyone comes to this church and preaches the simple gospel of Christ, believes in the power of prayer, and trusts in the Holy Spirit, this building will be full in no time.'[10]

In recent years I've been praying we'd see people come to faith in Christ every day in York. We've seen glimpses of this but we long for more, so we keep praying and working. Growth is God's desire for his church – that we grow in numbers, as well as in influence, maturity and impact. It's through the church that God wants to challenge evil powers of darkness[11] and it's through the church that he wants to impact the world.[12] Every disciple is called to be part of this.[13] John Wesley, the founder of Methodism, was right when he said, 'There is no such thing as solitary Christianity.' That's why it's important for disciples to be part of the family of the church.

If you don't belong to a local church, then join one. Look for a church that loves God, is full of the Holy Spirit, regularly celebrates the death and resurrection of Jesus (see **S is for Sacraments**), and wants to help people become his followers and impact their community. Pray and ask the Spirit to lead you to a vibrant church. He will. You certainly won't thrive and probably won't survive as a disciple outside church.

ACTION: If you're not part of a local church, resolve to join one and write about it in your notes. If you belong to a church, read Acts 2:42–47 and describe how you're helping to make your church increasingly like this first church. Then write down how you're receiving from your church and growing as a follower of Christ. Is there anything different you sense God wants you to do in order to better give to and receive from your church family?

PRAYER: Give thanks for the millions of local churches across the globe. Thank the Lord for the local churches in your village/town/city. Pray for your church leaders. Pray for growth in numbers, influence, maturity and impact.

D is for Disciplines

To excel in any field requires discipline. It's the same when it comes to discipleship. The ones that mature well and are most effective are the disciplined ones. In fact, one simple definition of 'disciple' is *disciplined one*. That's why **D is for Disciplines**.

Two crucial disciplines mentioned throughout this book are: regular reading of the Bible (see **B is for Bible**), and prayer (see **P is for Prayer**). To grow as a disciple, set aside time every day for those two disciplines. I've been doing that every day for over thirty years and it has been the most important aspect of my growth as a disciple. Daily devotional time like this will sustain you through the hard times and build strong foundations into your life.

There are many other disciplines mentioned in the Bible, including: meditation; study; simplicity; solitude; submission; rest; giving (see **G is for Giving**); service; confession; worship (see **W is for Worship**); guidance and celebration.[1] But of all the disciplines mentioned in the Bible, fasting stands out as one of the most basic and important. Most of the people used by God in the Bible and in the history of the church have fasted. That's because fasting particularly disciplines us and releases kingdom power (see **K is for Kingdom**). Some see it as a gateway into other disciplines and yet it's a much-neglected practice in many western churches. That's why this chapter focuses particularly on fasting as one of the key spiritual disciplines.

The Methodist movement, which I grew up in, helped bring revival to the UK and beyond when it began in the eighteenth and nineteenth centuries. Millions of lives were changed as the good news was proclaimed and demonstrated. People found faith in Christ, new churches were planted and the poor cared for. Part of the success was due to the discipline of its leaders and the insistence by Methodism's founder, John Wesley, that their ministers regularly fasted.[2]

I like to define fasting as *the voluntary giving up of food*.

It is *voluntary* in that it's a conscious choice. So if circumstances – like illness or a lack of food due to war or famine – force us to stop eating, that's not the kind of fasting described in the Bible. Fasting may well be motivated by the Holy Spirit, but in the end we're never forced to fast. It's a choice.

It is *giving up*. It involves stopping something. Saying 'no'. This is counter-intuitive as when we get hungry our bodies want to fill our stomachs. To deny feeding our hunger – even for a short period of time – can be a challenge, especially to those who aren't used to it. But the benefits can be great.

It normally involves not eating *food*. Eating food is basic to human nature; it's how we're made by God. Fasting involves deciding, for a time, not to eat food. Normally so we can pray (see **P is for Prayer**).

A few years ago I heard a leader from the church in Nigeria speaking about the outpouring of the Holy Spirit they were experiencing. He was asked why the church in the UK and Europe wasn't seeing such a move of God. His answer was simple and memorable: 'You don't know how to pray and fast.'

At The Belfrey we're just beginning to learn to fast. During January for the last two years the people of the church have been invited to join in a special period of Prayer and Fasting, to pray for awakening in our lives, our city and our region. Some fasted from food altogether, only drinking water. Some fasted from a meal each day (e.g. lunch), using that time instead to pray and listen to God. Some went on a 'Daniel Fast', eating only fruit and vegetables. And others fasted from something other than food, like social media.[3] Many spoke of how they had encountered the Lord and how he had profoundly spoken to them. Some of a particular closeness to his presence. Others of a new intimacy in worship. One woman who was fasting was asked by a friend what she was doing and consequently the friend (who was not yet a disciple) also decided to fast during the same period. At the end the friend said how he'd become more open and interested in the spiritual side of life and wanted to know more! These are some of the benefits that often come when we fast. We don't always see or know the consequences of our fasting, but we do know it's a good thing. God likes it.

That doesn't mean that fasting twists God's arm. And it certainly doesn't mean that fasting causes him to love us more, for our good Father can't love us any more or less. It just means that fasting is good.

Fasting is best practised both regularly and occasionally. In the early church, many fasted twice per week as part of their regular pattern of weekly devotions,[4] using the time when they would otherwise be eating to pray. Disciples should do the same today, finding a way to fast on a fairly regular basis. But fasting should also be practised occasionally – for a particular purpose. In the Bible we see people fasting in this way for a number of reasons, including: as a sign of humility;[5] a sign of repentance;[6] a sign of grief;[7] when seeking protection;[8] when seeking guidance;[9] when seeking healing;[10] when choosing leaders;[11] in preparation for spiritual warfare;[12] to avert war or national disaster;[13] for general spiritual growth.[14]

The Bible is full of characters who fasted, from Moses to the apostle Paul. And of course Jesus himself fasted.[15] Nowhere in the Bible does it suggest that fasting is part of the advanced manual for especially devout believers.[16] In fact when Jesus teaches on fasting in Matthew 6 he's giving basic discipleship teaching, placing it alongside his teaching on prayer that we now call 'the Lord's Prayer'. Fasting is normally meant for healthy adults and should not be imposed on babies, young children or the elderly or frail. Studies show that short periods of fasting are not detrimental to pregnant women or their unborn babies, but if in doubt on any medical matter a qualified doctor should be consulted. There's good medical evidence that fasting is beneficial to your body. The fact that most religions encourage fasting suggests that human beings have come to realize that it has further benefits too – not just for the body but also in sensitizing the soul.

The Bible teaches that the main aim of fasting should not be to lose weight but to help the disciple draw nearer to God. As such, fasting should not be divorced from loving God and loving people (see **L is for Love**). The prophet Isaiah is correct in teaching that it makes no sense to fast if we exploit others, are quarrelsome, are not standing up for justice, feeding the poor or caring for our families.[17]

If you're serious about being a disciple of Jesus, read the Bible and pray every day. In addition begin to embrace the ancient, powerful, but often neglected discipline of fasting. Also be ready for the Holy Spirit to open up new disciplines to you. He will. So you can be a disciple who highly impacts the world God has placed you in.

The great cellist William Pleeth was right, that 'behind great passion there must be great discipline'.[18]

ACTION: Are there any disciplines mentioned in this chapter that you're presently practising? If so, write them down. Are you yet noticing any benefit from them? Now focus on fasting, writing down the last time you chose to fast. If you've never fasted from food, don't worry; just make a decision to start (unless there's a medical reason why you shouldn't). Choose a day in the next week when you can miss a meal. Write it in your diary or on your calendar, so you don't forget. Resolve to use that time for prayer and reading the Bible, listening to God. Also listen to your body and its hunger for food. Turn that into a desire to hunger for God. Tell him you want more of him. Begin to learn to fast.

PRAYER: Ask the Spirit of God to lead you into greater depths of discipline. Ask him to keep your motives pure, so you're doing it to draw closer to him and see his kingdom come in greater measure – and for no other reason. Also ask him to bring you into contact with other disciples who are learning to be more disciplined (including fasting) so you can share experiences and grow together in a beautiful journey of disciplined discipleship.

E is for Encourage

My friend Ric is one of the most encouraging people I know. After spending time with him, I always feel uplifted. That's because he's an encourager. Some people, like Ric, are especially good at encouraging, but actually all disciples are called to encourage, as much and often as we can. That's why **E is for Encourage**.

We live in a world with much discouragement and disappointment. So much of the news is bad news and often quite depressing. Often the stories people like to tell are negative stories, criticizing their boss, the next-door neighbour, the football team or the government. If we join in with these negative stories we become part of the problem. We become discouragers. And followers of Jesus are not immune to this. We can so easily embrace the negativity that's in much of our culture and translate it into our lives, our workplaces, our families and churches. But disciples are called to something different. To encourage.[1] To build up. To speak well. To praise. To affirm. To be positive (see **Y is for Yes!**). We need to do this in every area of life,[2] creating a culture of honour in our homes and churches. Instead of being cynical, sceptical and pessimistic, disciples are called to honour one another,[3] encouraging children, friends, work colleagues, church and political leaders,[4] and everyone we come into contact with. That's why the Bible says, 'Encourage one other and build each other up'.[5]

There are at least fifty-nine 'one another' verses in the Bible. That means that fifty-nine times disciples are advised, urged and sometimes even commanded to do good things to or for or with one another – and they're all good and helpful things like love, forgive, greet and be patient. This reminds us that we all need each other and are called to share life together, helping and valuing each other.[6] We're not meant to be disciples on our own and we need each other in the encouraging community of the church (see **C is for Church**).[7]

In my own church I can think of many times when people have spoken a word of encouragement to me, or sent me a card or an encouraging email, just when I've been feeling low and really needed it. Following Jesus is sometimes hard, and while being a leader in the church is a great honour, there are times when it's particularly difficult and discouraging. Every leader knows this. That's why I've kept many of those cards and notes, and occasionally I get them out and read them, to encourage myself![8]

Encouraging each other doesn't mean that we never call people to account when they do something wrong.[9] It doesn't mean we ignore injustice, laziness or rudeness. It means that when we challenge and question, we do so with encouraging motives, acting kindly and politely, 'speaking the truth in love'[10] and wanting to build up the person we're challenging rather than tear them down. Such challenge is normally done privately rather than publicly (see **Q is for Quarrel**).

Mary and Martha are two female disciples who, along with their brother, encouraged Jesus by opening their home, befriending him, listening to his message and offering him hospitality.[11] This reminds us that being an encourager often involves doing something very practical. When Sam and I were first married and had very little money, we'd often invite friends over to eat with us. One friend, Clare, knew that our finances were tight and so she'd sometimes bring a practical gift, like a frozen chicken for the freezer or a packet of toilet roll for the bathroom. We were so encouraged!

Being an encourager often involves helping people see beyond their circumstances, helping them live above them rather than under them. Encouragers are people who know it's good 'to give thanks in all circumstances; for this is God's will for you in Christ Jesus'.[12] Encouragers are thankful, joyful people. Joy is about knowing a deep contentedness, whatever the circumstances.[13] Joy strengthens us[14] and results in thankfulness. Disciples can be thankful at all times. Even when things are tough and we're feeling tired.[15] Even when things happen that we don't understand and we're feeling uncertain.[16] Even in mourning when loved ones die and we're feeling sad.[17] There are always things to be thankful for.[18]

When we encourage individuals it's important that we praise not just good behaviour but people's identities. Whether the person we're addressing is a follower of Christ or not, it's a wonderful thing to play a part in strengthening good character and identity. When we do that, we frustrate the devil, who loves to make people insecure in their identity.[19] However, our Heavenly Father calls us to join with him in helping people become more confident in who they are (see **I is for Identity**). This is particularly important in children, but also in adults. So it's great to be told 'You're good at music' but even better to hear 'You're a good musician.' It's affirming to be told 'You communicated that really clearly' but even better to be told 'You're a clear communicator.'

Barnabas is a Bible character who many disciples have found to be a great source of inspiration when it comes to encouragement. His very name means 'son of encouragement'.[20] He was a generous person (see **G is for Giving**), was 'glad' and 'encouraged' others,[21] partly by telling stories – testimonies – of God's work. Testimonies are a great source of encouragement, building love and faith (see **F is for Faith**). Barnabas is also described as 'a good man, full of the Holy Spirit and faith'.[22] His desire was to be used by God to help others become disciples[23] and to see the church built up in love and faith and to impact the world. What a great example of an encourager he is.

But the best role model of all is Jesus Christ. He was an even better encourager than Barnabas! In all that he did, with everyone he met, he sought to encourage. As we, his disciples, are filled with his Spirit today, so we're called to change the world by being the most encouraging people on planet earth.

What a calling! What an honour!

ACTION: Write down the names of anyone you've encouraged over the last week. Then write down the names of three people you will probably meet today who you could encourage in some way.

PRAYER: Now pray for opportunities today to encourage these three people. Pray too for the ability to affirm and praise their identities (e.g. 'You're a really good listener/baker/leader.').

F is for Faith

Faith is seeing the unseen, believing it's true and then living in the light of it.[1] It takes faith to get in an aeroplane and fly in the sky – especially for the first time. You might wonder how a metal object that's heavier than air will defy gravity and take you safely to your destination. To fly takes faith. But given that planes fly all over the world every day and we see people around us who regularly travel this way, this faith is based on good evidence. Nevertheless some faith is required! Similarly faith is required to become a disciple, and to go on as a disciple. That's why **F is for Faith**.

It takes faith to become a disciple of Jesus. There's an initial step of faith, as we say 'yes' to God. We don't fully know the outcome. We might have read a little of the Bible and understood a few things about Jesus and what he's done. We might know others who are believers who have something about them we find attractive. We don't know everything, but we see enough to step out and begin to follow. That stepping out is an act of faith.

God loves faith. He loves to respond to it.[2] When he sees someone exercising faith he is stirred. I love bacon and the smell of it cooking. If I smell bacon in the house I can't help but be drawn to it. It gets my attention. God is like that with faith. He loves it! It gets his attention.

We don't need much faith for God to respond. Our Father senses the little bit of faith we're exercising and acts. Jesus made this very clear to his followers, saying that we only need faith 'as small as a mustard seed' for God to move mountains![3] What's most important is not that we have great faith but that we have faith in a great God. That's why in Luke 17 Jesus answers the disciples' request for more faith by encouraging them to be faithful and obedient (see **O is for Obedience**).[4] That means that faith is not just something we exercise as we begin to follow Jesus. Being a disciple is a life of faith. We begin in faith and go on in faith. Some disciples forget this. They start well but stop exercising faith or growing in faith. Don't let that happen. Instead embrace the journey of faith and keep asking the Holy Spirit to lead you and stretch your faith, day by day.

The Bible says that faith comes as we hear God's word.[5] His word in Scripture speaks to our hearts, releasing faith, whether we sense it or not. This word brings us to new birth (see **N is for New**), enabling us to see more and more of God's kingdom.[6] As we read the Bible daily and regularly (see **B is for Bible**) it helps us grow in faith. When we receive a prophetic word which speaks specifically to our lives, it can have the same effect (see **H is for Holy Spirit**). In fact we cannot come to faith or grow in faith without God's word working in us. Faith is like yeast, activating the dough of God's word and causing it to grow in us.[7]

Abraham is someone described in the Bible as the 'father' of faith.[8] So if you want to grow in faith, read Abraham's story.[9] After an encounter with God he stepped out and obeyed God, having been told to get up and move to a different land. He didn't even know where he was going but faithfully obeyed God's word. If you want to be inspired by examples of faith, read Hebrews chapter 11 which gives multiple examples of men and women who exercised faith. It's a great read! As we get to know their stories, so we're motivated to live by faith.

Telling encouraging stories is very important when it comes to faith. That's why Psalm 107:1–2 says:

Give thanks to the LORD, for he is good;
his love endures for ever.
Let the redeemed of the LORD tell their story . . .

There's great power in thankful testimony. As we read stories of faith in the Bible and hear stories of faith today, so the Holy Spirit stirs our hearts, fills us with joy and builds our faith.

At The Belfrey in York we find that baptisms generate more baptisms. This is because those who aren't yet Christians see women and men putting their faith in Jesus, hear their stories and the difference Christ has made, and it results in them seeing an alternative future for their lives – believing this can happen to them. Testimony does this. It's an opportunity for God to do it again.[10] When faith stories are told – for example about financial provision, or marriage restoration or healing – people believe that God can do the same thing for them, or for a friend or loved one, and this can be a catalyst for the Holy Spirit to bring transformation. Sometimes people get healed as the story is told, even without anyone praying for them! My colleague Greg Downes was recently telling a story in a sermon about a woman he'd prayed with who, after an encounter with God, found she could now sleep through the night. Listening to his sermon was another woman who'd been similarly struggling with insomnia for over a year since being involved in a sleep study which had disrupted her sleep pattern. As the second woman heard how the first was healed, she knew there and then she was healed. No one prayed for her. She simply felt faith arise in her and knew God had healed her. She met Greg a few days later to tell him that since hearing that story in the sermon she had slept perfectly. Such is the power of testimony. Testimony releases faith.

When human beings exercise faith, it's always faith in something or someone. Sometimes people put their faith in an insurance policy, in a religious system, in another person, or even in themselves. But disciples are called to put their faith primarily in God. The God who's revealed himself in Jesus Christ (see **J is for Jesus**), who fills us by his Spirit (see **H is for Holy Spirit**) and who is a good Father (see **A is for Abba**). As we trust in the goodness of God – even when circumstances seem to challenge the idea that God is good – so God responds by providing all the resources of the kingdom of heaven needed for the situation (see **K is for Kingdom**). When life is tough, it's particularly important to tell the stories of what God has done in the past – in others and in us – so our perspective is renewed and faith built.

Faith, as we're seeing, involves seeing the unseen. We glimpse a different future. So instead of seeing an alcoholic whose life is wasting away, faith enables us to see someone sober and rebuilding their life. Instead of seeing a declining church, faith enables us to see a growing, vibrant church, impacting the locality. Instead of seeing a devastated community high in crime and with boarded-up properties, faith enables us to see a regenerated, healthy, prosperous community, full of kindness, where everyone wants to live. Such is the power of faith. A faith that stirs us to action.

Sometimes God gives faith to people for a particular moment, or for certain things, or for something in the future, enabling us to persevere (see **O is for Obedience**). Sometimes I find faith rising in me as I pray for something or someone. I can see the outcome and I know I'm praying with faith. Normally those prayers are answered. When praying for individuals, I particularly have faith when it comes to finding jobs and houses. As a result I see lots of answers to prayers for those things. Of course I'll pray for all sorts of other things and often God answers those prayers too (see **P is for Prayer**). Sometimes I know that certain things are going to happen, especially if the Lord has spoken to me previously in prayer or in a dream (see **H is for Holy Spirit**). I have faith. In the long term I have faith that the Lord is going to visit the north of England with an outpouring of his Spirit. I don't know if it will be sudden or slow. But I believe it's going to happen. I can see it. I believe it's true. And I'm seeking to live in the light of it.

God wants disciples to grow in faith.[11] This happens as we learn to trust him more, day by day. This involves stepping out and not relying on ourselves but on him. Anything that happens in his kingdom is his work, not ours. He uses us and uses our faith, which is a great honour. But the work is his. And so the glory is his. That's why, when God uses our faith to do wonderful and sometimes seemingly impossible things,[12] we give thanks to our Father for all his goodness.

F is for Faith

ACTION: If faith is seeing the future, believing what you see and acting on it, when was the last time you exercised faith? Write it down. What about your faith in Jesus Christ? Have you consciously chosen to put your faith in Jesus Christ, and begun following him? If not, what's stopping you? Is today the day to begin? If yes, what is the Lord showing you that you need to act on? Is there a situation in your life where you think God has shown you the future and what you need to do, but you're fearful of exercising faith? Write it down.

PRAYER: Now turn all these things to prayer. Ask the Holy Spirit to fill you and give you courage to believe and act. Ask him to build your faith today, as you begin to follow Jesus, in faith, or go on following Jesus.

G is for Giving

God's love for us is absolutely wonderful. The Bible has a special word for it: 'grace'.[1] Grace is a love that's undeserved, unconditional and unending.[2] God's grace is offered freely to every single person on the planet in Jesus Christ.[3] Who wouldn't want to be loved like that?

Because grace is free to receive, it's also free to give.[4] Disciples are called to give like God[5] – generously and graciously.[6] That's why **G is for Giving**.

My family and I have known many times when our good Father has generously given to us, especially through other disciples. We've been given food on the doorstep (such as eggs, potatoes, rhubarb, chocolate cake and doughnuts), holidays and even a car – and we've done the same for others. While there've been times when our finances have been tight, we've always had enough – in fact *more* than enough, enabling us to give too. That's what the Bible says – that God provides more than enough resources so we can share.[7] Even when we've felt at the end of our resources, we've always found, as we've dug deep, that we've had more than enough love to give, forgiveness to share, food to eat, clothes to wear and money in our pockets – so we can live and give.

When I was vicar of St Chad's Church in Sheffield our house was located next door to the church and known by many in our community as 'the vicarage'. As a result we'd often get people coming to our door asking for help. We loved to help, although we'd taken a decision years before that if people asked for money we'd politely say 'no' (as it too often ended up funding and perpetuating an addiction), but we'd always offer something, like food or practical help and a prayer. Sometimes this meant topping up an electricity meter, buying a bus or train ticket, or driving someone somewhere. It also meant that our cupboards sometimes were cleared out of things like rice and pasta, tins of soup, and bread and tea – and we'd have to go shopping again to stock up. At times it was tight and we had to trust God, but we were never, ever, short.

We've always sought to do the same with our financial giving, believing that while all resources come from God, the first 10% is always his without any need for asking and goes to the local church (see **C is for Church**). This is called 'tithing'. Tithing is a principle encouraged in both the Old and New Testaments.[8] Malachi 3:10 promises that tithing benefits not just the recipient but also the giver – and even urges believers to 'test [God] in this'. We've done that and he's never let us down. In fact I've given at least a tithe of my income to my church since I was 19 years old and I believe God has always honoured this giving. That's why I urge all disciples to give at least a tithe of their income to their local church. Sam and I now give more than a tithe to our church and aim to give more each year than the one before. On top of that, we also support other good causes, including the education of two children from poorer nations and the work of a few chosen charities and individuals. We've also had people come to live with us from time to time who are in need. We don't do so begrudgingly but gladly and joyfully.[9] It's good for us and good for others. It's all part of discipleship.

The Bible says that as disciples generously give, so God will be generous back to us, so we can give again. You can read about it in 2 Corinthians 9:6–11 as well as Proverbs 11:24. This is the radical economics of the kingdom of God (see **K is for Kingdom**) which at times stretches our faith (see **F is for Faith**) but is always good.

A number of women are mentioned in the gospel accounts as 'helping to support [Jesus and his disciples] out of their own means'.[10] They are named as Mary Magdalene, Joanna and Susanna and, because they're mentioned in the Bible, they're forever remembered for their generous giving. All disciples – not just female followers of Jesus – are called to a lifestyle of giving.[11]

Of course living a life based on giving is about much more than money: it's about being generous in speech, in time, in love, in prayer – in fact, in *every* area of life. Jesus modelled this beautifully for us, and his Spirit will help us to live generously like Christ, as we ask him. However, generous giving mustn't exclude our finances – and some disciples in the West find this particularly taxing(!). The fear of not having enough is strong and needs to be acknowledged and broken by exercising generous giving to the church and to others.

Adam Grant has shown from secular empirical research that living as a giver and being part of a generous community is the best way for all human beings to live.[12] Not only does it change the world but it also benefits and satisfies the giver, as long as they don't become a doormat in the process and look after their own mental and emotional well-being. This agrees with the message of the Bible.

Sometimes people ask me how much they should give. The answer is that generosity can't be quantified. Giving £20 might indeed be generous for someone living on benefits, but it's probably not for someone earning £20,000 per year.[13] That's why, in the end, we need to be honest and at peace with God and with ourselves about how much we give. It's good to remember that generous disciples never lie on their deathbeds longing that they'd given less! If anything, they wish they'd given even more, because they know that Jesus meant it when he said: 'Give, and it will be given to you. A good measure, pressed down, shaken together and running over, will be poured into your lap. For with the measure you use, it will be measured to you.'[14]

ACTION: Is there a particular situation known to you which would benefit from your generosity? If so, resolve to do something to help today. Are you giving to your local church? If not, start to do that. It will benefit not just the church but you too. If you're not sure, read Malachi 3:8–12 and start to give regularly.

PRAYER: It's sometimes said that 'you can't outgive God', so ask the Lord to expand your vision of him and to see his gracious, generous, giving nature more and more clearly. Then write down a prayer to God, asking him to help you not just to give occasionally but to be a giving person.

H is for Holy Spirit

The Holy Spirit is 'God's empowering presence'.[1] He is God with us today. He is not a force but a person, which is why the Bible describes him as 'he' rather than 'it'. He works inside and outside the church, establishing the kingdom of God. He particularly desires for people to be immersed in him – baptized and drenched in him – so the world can be soaked in his presence. Being full of the Holy Spirit is essential to being an effective disciple. That's why **H is for Holy Spirit**.

When I was 18 years old I became increasingly hungry for more of God. I'd decided to follow Christ in my early teens and during my secondary school years was part of a profound move of God in my school, which saw a good number of my friends become believers. I knew God's Spirit was with me but I also realized there was much more of God to experience and I wanted to be increasingly fruitful for him. So I sought God, in prayer and through reading Scripture. I went to university in the city of Nottingham and found a church where the Spirit of God was at work. The following months were then very formative for me. I had a number of encounters with the Holy Spirit which resulted in a new love for the Bible, a release in worship and adoration, speaking in tongues,[2] and a growing confidence in hearing his prophetic voice. God was filling and baptizing me in his Holy Spirit.

I've subsequently learned that being immersed in the Holy Spirit isn't meant to be just a one-off experience but a regular occurrence[3] as part of my ongoing relationship with Christ.[4] Like all disciples, I need to be full to overflowing with the Father's love. Fullness is measured by overflow and impact. If I'm making little impact with my life, I need to be filled and baptized with the Holy Spirit.

The Spirit is God himself – the third person of the Trinity (see **T is for Trinity**) – and is often described with the prefix 'Holy'. This word 'holy' means 'godlike' or 'godly', encapsulating all aspects of the nature and attributes of God, from his power and perfection to his love and mercy. When we encounter the Holy Spirit we therefore encounter holiness. One of his roles is to help disciples and the church become more holy and godlike.[5] This often involves conviction of sin[6] and empowering us to repent (see **R is for Repentance**) and turn away from wrongdoing and live lives of love and service. This means that living a holy life is not just a matter of human effort. Rather the Spirit wants to help us and fill us, so we become more and more like Jesus, bearing his fruit (see **J is for Jesus**).[7] In the same way that a hand fills a glove, enabling the glove to no longer be limp but to fulfil its purpose, so the Holy Spirit wants to fill human beings so we can fulfil God's purposes for our lives.

The Holy Spirit is the Spirit of Jesus.[8] He's the same Spirit who filled Jesus,[9] who empowered him to live as our model for the Spirit-filled life, and then raised him from the dead.[10] He's the Spirit who sets people free from all that binds,[11] bringing liberty.[12] Jesus chose to rely on the Spirit, walk in the Spirit, and work in the power of the Spirit. Jesus was a temple for the Holy Spirit. Disciples are called to be the same.[13]

The Holy Spirit is the Spirit of creativity,[14] present at creation,[15] and the One who brings fresh life, renewing the earth.[16]

The first person in the Bible described as 'full of the Spirit' was a craftsman, inspired by the Spirit of God to make beautiful things.[17] The Holy Spirit continues to birth new initiatives and inspires creative ideas and abilities in people (see **N is for New**).

The Holy Spirit is not confined to the church. He is the life and dynamic of the kingdom of God (see **K is for Kingdom**) and so also works outside the church, affecting people, circumstances, institutions, governments and nations. However, he particularly loves to work in people who are committed to Christ and actively seeking his presence.[18] He loves to work in the church and overflow out of the church, bringing cultural change and revival.[19]

The Holy Spirit loves to be invited,[20] which is why one of the most ancient prayers of the church is 'Come, Holy Spirit.' To invoke and welcome the Spirit doesn't mean that he was not present before. It simply means we are asking him to come in greater measure, manifesting his presence to a greater degree.

The Holy Spirit loves to give gifts to God's people. He distributes the good gifts of our gracious Father. These can be both natural and supernatural gifts. The Bible says that we should seek and desire his gifts.[21]

The Holy Spirit loves to give wisdom to people. If you want to live wisely, the Bible says you 'should ask God, who gives generously to all without finding fault, and it will be given to you'.[22] In some parts of the Old Testament wisdom is personified, described as 'she'.[23] Many theologians have suggested that she is the Holy Spirit and they're probably right, which is why the apostle Paul prays for 'the Spirit of wisdom and revelation' to be given to Christ-followers.[24] Disciples need this wisdom. Wisdom to know God better.[25] Wisdom to explain what it means to be a disciple of Jesus to those who are not yet following him.[26] Wisdom to live well in a mixed-up world.[27] Wisdom to know the difference between good and best.[28] Wisdom to lead well.[29] Wisdom to solve difficult problems.[30] Wisdom to invent and innovate.[31] Wisdom to create beauty – in worship, in our homes and communities.[32] Wisdom that helps people become caught up in the wonder of God's goodness. World leaders also need wisdom – perhaps more than any other commodity. Disciples are called to pray for them[33] and for this wisdom that comes from the Holy Spirit.

The Holy Spirit loves to give discernment to disciples. Wisdom is a general gift whereas discernment is more specific, helping us apply wisdom in a particular context. You can have wisdom without discernment, but you can't have discernment without wisdom.[34] Such discernment requires us to be listening to our good Father. As we listen, God often communicates a particular message to us. The Bible calls this 'prophecy'. The Lord has much to say to disciples, to build us up and encourage us.[35] We're told to 'eagerly desire . . . prophecy',[36] which means we should seek to hear God communicating to us not just through Scripture but also through things like words, pictures and dreams. When God speaks like this, it's good to go through a threefold process of discernment, considering the *revelation*, the *interpretation* and the *application*.

The *revelation* is about understanding the content of the word/dream/picture. Here you're asking 'What is the message?' When it comes to *interpretation* you're asking 'What is the meaning?' There may be lots of potential meanings of the revelation you've received. Discernment is needed. Then *application* is required, where you ask 'What do I do with this?' It's good to consider: is this a message for me, or someone else? Is this simply to encourage me and for prayer, or is there something practical for me to do? If it's particularly significant and/or seems to suggest a change in direction, you should expect the Spirit to confirm this (usually a number of times) and often through other people. None of this should contradict Scripture and should be tested.[37] If you're new to prophecy there are all sorts of books that can be read and courses to go on, to learn to discern the voice of the Holy Spirit.

Most of all, the Holy Spirit loves to bring the Father's love (see **A is for Abba** and **L is for Love**).[38] He loves the Father and the Son, and seeks to do all he can to honour them. He loves the plans and purposes of God.[39] He loves the world. He loves the church.[40] He loves to fill disciples with the love of God,[41] so they can fulfil Jesus' Great Commandment, to love God and love others.[42] When we are short of love, we need the Holy Spirit. He is the Spirit of love.

ACTION: Having read today's chapter, search your heart and write down any thoughts and desires that are particularly stirring in you regarding the Holy Spirit. Do you want to be immersed in the Holy Spirit (either for the first time, or again)? Is there a particular gift you would like to ask for? Ask yourself, 'What would I like the Holy Spirit to do in me?' Write down your answers.

PRAYER: Now turn your answers to these questions into prayer. Spend some time asking the Holy Spirit to come and fill you and answer your prayers. Give some space and time for this, and welcome his presence. He longs to fill you. To overflowing. Pray: 'Come, Holy Spirit.'

☐ is for Identity

People in twenty-first-century western society are desperately searching for identity. Many try to find their identity through their work. We often encourage this when our opening question to someone is asking what they do. But for the disciple of Jesus things are different. Disciples find their identity not in what they do but in Christ. Being secure in your relationship with God is essential to being an effective disciple. This is why **I is for Identity**.

Identity is about who I am. Nicky Gumbel rightly says that 'Your age doesn't define your maturity; your grades don't define your ability; and what people say about you doesn't define who you are.'[1] Rather, a disciple's identity is shaped by who God is and what he says – and it's sealed at baptism.[2]

God the Father spoke to Jesus in an identity-defining encounter at his baptism. We read about it in Matthew 3:17. At Jesus' baptism, not only was he immersed in the Spirit but the Father spoke from heaven, affirming three things about his identity, saying 'This is my Son, whom I love; with him I am well pleased.' When we're baptized, God the Father says exactly the same three things to us.

First, he wants us to realize that we're his sons and daughters and have been adopted into a new family – *his* family. As he is the Great King, that means that we are of royal status.[3] Rather than being insignificant, we have dignity and favour. Protection and provision. We can be confident and courageous. We can hold our head high as we have a great and noble inheritance.

Second, the Father wants to assure us that we're loved (see **L is for Love**). Deeply, profoundly, kindly and generously. Rather than allowing us to feel unloved, the Father wants us to know that he created us to love us, and sent his Son to die for us, because of his great love.[4] The identity of every disciple, then, is rooted in the love of God.[5] It's this gracious love that has transferred us from the realm of darkness – that is, from a world of serving ourselves – into his kingdom of light[6] – serving the one true God – which liberates us.

Third, the Father wants us to know that he's pleased with us. The Father was pleased with Jesus not because of what he'd done (as his baptism came before he began any teaching or miracles) but on the basis of who Jesus was – simply his child. And it's the same for us. Rather than being overlooked, we are seen by God and he delights in us! If the Father's pleasure was based on our performance we would all have grounds for being insecure, but thankfully this isn't the case. Instead, every disciple can know that God takes great pleasure in them. That's how I feel about my children, despite me and them being imperfect – so how much more does God take pleasure in us!

So baptism marks a change in identity for the follower of Jesus. That's why disciples are baptized people. In fact baptism is the main sign of being a follower of Jesus (see **S is for Sacraments**).

The more disciples see, believe and live in the light of their true identity, the more mature they become and the more impact they have. That's why the Holy Spirit loves to regularly remind us of who we are, in Christ. Conversely the Bible says we have an enemy who likes to undermine who we are. He's the same enemy Jesus had – the devil – Satan.[7] He is not going to win, as he has already been fatally defeated by Christ on the cross[8] and his destiny is clear.[9] However, he still fights on until the end of time with his demonic forces, seeking 'to steal and kill and destroy'.[10]

Disciples need not fear the devil but he should be resisted,[11] fought against not with physical aggression[12] but with prayer,[13] humble living[14] and loving those who are against us.[15] Jesus called him 'the father of lies',[16] and one significant way he lies is by challenging disciples over this issue of identity, because if he can make us believe we're insignificant, unloved and over-looked he knows we'll be ineffective. He often does this im-mediately after baptism or an encounter with God, as he did with Jesus,[17] and we shouldn't be surprised if the same happens to us. So disciples need to be aware of the enemy's plan[18] and realize that when we think we're excluded from (rather than included in) God's family, or are despised (rather than loved) by God, or that God is enraged (rather than pleased) with us, we are wrong. Those thoughts are lies. They don't come from God. Such challenges need to be countered with the truth of Scripture (see **B is for Bible**) as we're reminded of who God is and who we are. As Ben Doolan, my friend and colleague at The Belfrey, says: 'The adversary points at our performance; the Advocate points at our position.'[19]

When we're challenged over our identity we can know that God gives us all the resources of heaven so we come out stronger, not weaker, and more empowered by the Spirit, not less.[20] That's what happened to Jesus in his so-called *temptations*. So we have nothing to fear.

As part of the community of the church (see **C for Church**), we don't need to go through such battles on our own, but can face them with others. Don't forget that through the death and resurrection of Jesus we've been adopted into a *family*. A good family. A family whose members look out for each other and are called to support, care and encourage one another (see **E is for Encourage**). We bear the family name – the name of Christ. We stand in his name. We love in his name. We pray in his name. We have authority in his name. That means that the new identity that we're given when we become followers of Jesus is not just a personal thing, but corporate. Together we are 'a chosen people, a royal priesthood, a holy nation'.[21] This is who we are. In Christ. Because of Christ.

Occasionally a body of believers will begin to grasp the significance of their corporate identity. As I've travelled internationally I've seen it when visiting various locations. When the church gathers for worship there's a culture of expectation, that people are going to encounter God there and then. Invariably they do and the testimonies shared are often moving. When they disperse, the church is encouraged to live in the light of their God-given royal identity, and as a result God's presence is experienced not inside church but outside – in homes, schools, workplaces and shopping arcades. This is what happens when disciples of Christ together arise and embrace their new identity as baptized people, immersed in the Spirit.

Disciples don't need to go looking for their identity. It's already been given by God in Christ. Instead disciples are called as baptized people to know who they've become. Know that, and the world will be transformed.

ACTION: God the Father says: 'You are my son/daughter, whom I love; with you I am well pleased.' That means God has 1) adopted you into his family, 2) poured his love into you and 3) is pleased with you. Spend some time considering these three areas, and ask whether you believe each one, and if so, what the implications are for you. Write down your reflections.

PRAYER: If you're not yet a disciple, would you like to have this change of identity? Does anything concern you? What questions do you still have? If you're already a disciple, thank God for the new identity you have. Ask him to help you to believe this more and to live in the light of it today, bringing his transforming love into every situation. Pray for an area of the world where disciples of Jesus are persecuted, asking the Spirit of Jesus to strengthen their identity and resolve, and to help them courageously witness for Christ today.

J is for Jesus

Although we've considered some aspects of the person of Jesus already in this *A–Z of Discipleship*, **J is for Jesus**. You see, it doesn't take long for a disciple to realize that you just can't get enough of Jesus! In fact every chapter in this book includes something about him. That's because there are always more wonderful things to discover about Jesus Christ.

I've found this to be true in my own life. The more I seek Christ, the more I discover. The more I discover, the more I'm amazed.

You can read about Jesus. Study Jesus. Think about Jesus. Meet people who know a lot about Jesus. But the best way to get to know Jesus is to begin a relationship with him. Just begin talking with him and living your life with him. In him. Immersed in him. As you do this, you'll find a growing love for him, as the Holy Spirit draws you to him in a relationship of friendship and love.[1]

On my last Sunday as vicar of St Chad's Church in Sheffield, before moving to York, we baptized more people than we'd ever baptized before. It was a moving service. One person I helped baptize was a lady who lived locally and had begun coming to church about eighteen months before. For many weeks she would slip in quietly just after we'd begun and sit at the back and weep through most of the service, especially through the worship. I went to chat with her a number of times in those first few months. I remember her asking if it was OK for her to be there. I reassured her it was. I asked about her tears. She said they were not tears of anguish but good tears, tears that felt right and were somehow tears of healing. I said that she was responding to the presence of Jesus, the One who loved her. Over the coming months she came to know this Jesus. This kind, caring, forgiving Saviour. And on my final Sunday in Sheffield she was immersed in the waters of baptism, marking her new-found love for Jesus.

Disciples of Jesus love Jesus. We love him because he first loved us.[2] And he still keeps loving us. Day after day after day. And he will keep doing so. For the rest of our lives and into eternity.[3] That's incredible! That's why John Stott called him 'the incomparable Christ'.[4]

The Russian writer Dostoevsky similarly said: 'I believe there is no-one lovelier, deeper, more sympathetic, and more perfect than Jesus. I say to myself, with jealous love, that not only is there no-one else like him, but there could never be anyone like him.'[5] I honestly believe that Dostoevsky is right. Jesus is utterly fantastic! Brilliantly wonderful! And much more. Here are a few reasons why:

Jesus perfectly shows us what God is like.[6] He was God in human form[7] – 100% divine yet also 100% human (not 50% divine and 50% human). He loved, cared, forgave and healed people.[8] He spoke wise and inspirational words of truth, grace and hope (that we can read about in the gospels: Matthew, Mark, Luke and John). He faced opposition, ridicule and accusation but never took offence.[9] He particularly cared for the vulnerable, hurting and marginalized[10] and gave his all to see lives changed.[11] He invited people to follow him[12] and by doing so to enter into the kingdom of God[13] which he proclaimed and demonstrated. Jesus changed the world through love – expressing this most perfectly and profoundly by voluntarily dying a horrendous death by crucifixion[14] through which sin, death and the devil were defeated.[15] To demonstrate this, God the Father raised Jesus from the dead and after forty days he ascended to heaven[16] from where he poured out the Holy Spirit on his disciples,[17] so they could experience the ongoing and indwelling presence of Christ and continue to see God's kingdom come on earth as in heaven.[18] Jesus now reigns in heaven,[19] seated on his royal throne at the right hand of his Father,[20] and from that place of honour and victory he gives himself to pray for us until the end of human time, for God's purposes to be fulfilled on earth.[21]

Jesus both knows and values what it is to be human, sharing the same kinds of experiences that most of us have – including the good and the bad. As he grew up in his family he'd have experienced joy, laughter, love, hard work, good food and fine storytelling, while also seeing suffering, poverty, oppression and injustice through living in a nation (Israel) occupied by a victorious enemy (Rome) and its soldiers. He was tempted in the same way we are and yet he never sinned.[22] He knew he was loved by his Father and was secure in his identity,[23] appropriately exercising the authority given him in the Spirit.[24] As such, he is the perfect role model and there is no one better to follow.[25]

The name 'Jesus' comes from the Hebrew word 'Joshua' which means 'saviour, rescuer, hero'.[26] His name summarizes so much about his identity. However, to help us see how wonderful Christ is, the Bible includes other names and terms that express who he is and what he's done. These include: Immanuel ('God with us');[27] the Son of God;[28] the Son of Man;[29] Prince of Peace;[30] Lion of Judah;[31] Lamb of God;[32] Wonderful Counsellor;[33] Master;[34] Light of the World;[35] Chief Cornerstone;[36]

Holy One;[37] King of Kings;[38] Head of the Church;[39] the Word of God;[40] Bread of Life;[41] Good Shepherd;[42] Resurrection and Life;[43] True Vine;[44] Way, Truth and Life;[45] Rock;[46] High Priest;[47] Lord of All;[48] True God;[49] Alpha and Omega;[50] Lord.[51]

Disciples are followers of this Jesus but also his ambassadors.[52] That means that we represent him – wherever we go and whatever we do. This is both a tremendous privilege and a great responsibility. As we represent him he gives us his power and authority, which we're to use in his name.[53] That's why disciples often end their prayers 'in the name of Jesus'[54] and why proclamations, declarations, healings and deliverances are normally given 'in the name of Jesus'.[55] Disciples know that Jesus Christ is the King of the kingdom of God and that one day in the future he will return for a second time.[56] He will come to rule and judge, and there will be a day when 'at the name of Jesus every knee [will] bow'.[57] In anticipation of that day disciples bow the knee now, and recognize the lordship of Jesus Christ.[58] Filled with his Spirit, in our work and witness we humbly but boldly invite others to do the same.[59] For there is no one like Christ.[60] No one comes close to him. No one ever will. He is the Saviour of the World.[61]

ACTION: Read again some of the names of Jesus listed in this chapter and write down three of them which particularly stand out to you. Think about why you've chosen these three names. Look up the Bible verses related to them. Speak out these names a few times so you can learn them.

PRAYER: Now speak out these three names again, but this time as worship, directed to Christ. Thank Jesus for who he is and what he's done. Then ask the Lord for opportunities today to point people to Jesus and to express to someone who doesn't know him just how amazing he is. Ask the Spirit to lead you in this. Be expectant today that he will.

K is for Kingdom

The kingdom of God is the central and unifying theme of Jesus' message. Jesus initiated the kingdom, preached about the kingdom, demonstrated the kingdom and invited people to enter into the kingdom. Disciples of Jesus are called to do exactly the same, working and praying for God's heavenly kingdom to come here on earth. That's why **K is for Kingdom**.

Bill Johnson helpfully describes praying for the kingdom of God like this:

> When we pray, 'Thy kingdom come, Thy will be done,' we're praying for the King's dominion and will to be realized right here, right now. That is a life-transforming, paradigm-shattering way to 'do' normal Christianity. God has not kept His desires secret: He wants the reality of heaven to invade this rebel-torn world, to transform it, to bring it under His headship. What is free to operate in heaven – joy, peace, wisdom, health, wholeness, and all the other good promises we read about in the Bible – should be free to operate here on this planet, in your home, your church, your business, and your school . . .
>
> When we make this our mission, lives are set free, bodies are restored, darkness lifts from people's minds, the rule of the enemy is pushed back in every way imaginable. Businesses grow healthy, relationships flower again, people re-connect with their calling and purpose in life, churches grow, and cities feel the effects of having the kingdom flourishing within them. Energy is freed up

for kingdom works in ways I have never seen before. Things happen regularly that are so extraordinary it's like stepping into the pages of a good novel. But it's not a made-up lifestyle; it's the lifestyle for which we were made.[1]

People have used phrases such as 'kingship of God', 'divine government' and 'reign of God' to summarize what Jesus meant by his kingdom. While these are of some help, I find an easy way to think of the kingdom is simply this: God's kingdom is anywhere Jesus is at work.

When Jesus began his work (see **J is for Jesus**) he made a bold and simple declaration, saying: 'The time has come! . . . The kingdom of God has come near. Repent and believe the good news!'[2] He was telling people that because he was present and at work, so was his kingdom. With the coming of Christ the kingdom comes near to people.[3] It's the same kingdom described in Isaiah 61 (which Jesus quotes in Luke 4:16–21) – a place of salvation, freedom, healing and deliverance. Whenever we see these things, we are seeing signs of Christ present and at work, bringing the kingdom of his Father[4] in the power of the Spirit.[5]

Jesus told his followers that they too should work and pray that the 'kingdom [would] come . . . on earth as it is in heaven'.[6] This tells us that the fullness of the kingdom is found in heaven. One day in eternity we'll see it and experience this kingdom totally.[7] It will be truly wonderful! It will be a place of no sin, sickness or suffering.[8] That's why, when Jesus commissions disciples to carry out kingdom work this side of heaven, it includes a call for people to receive his forgiveness, his healing and his peace.[9] Jesus says that as disciples seek first this kingdom, there's no need to worry about our everyday material needs.[10]

One of my favourite times of the week at The Belfrey is when we share testimonies at our weekly Staff Morning. I love to encourage us to share stories of where we've seen recent signs of the kingdom. Sometimes we hear great stories of conversions and healings and miraculous provision. But we also cherish the seemingly smaller things – like someone being brave and inviting a friend to church or an Alpha course, or someone having a go at something for the first time. These testimonies build our faith (see **F is for Faith**). God loves them all as they're all examples of his kingdom coming here on earth, as in heaven.

Disciples co-labour with God[11] in building his kingdom, often in very practical ways. Theologian Tom Wright expresses it like this:

What you do in the present – by painting, preaching, singing, sewing, praying, teaching, building hospitals, digging wells, campaigning for justice, writing poems, caring for the needy, loving your neighbour as yourself – will last into God's future. These activities are not simply ways of making the present life a little less beastly, a little more bearable, until the day when we leave it behind altogether. They are part of what we may call building for God's kingdom.[12]

Some people talk of 'the now and not yet' of God's kingdom. By that they mean that we see signs and glimpses of the kingdom now, but there'll be much more – the 'not yet' – which we'll only see fully in heaven. To think in this way can be helpful. However, it's possible to use the 'not yet' idea as an excuse for not pursuing more of God's kingdom today. We must take care not to do that as Jesus was clear that we're to pray, seek and pursue the kingdom *now*. Disciples must keep asking themselves: how much more of God's kingdom can I see in my life? In my family? In my church? In my community? In my nation? The answer is always: 'much more'! And that should be our motive for persevering and seeking more of God's kingdom.

Often when I'm praying for healing for people, they improve but they're not fully healed. I've learned to keep going and pray for more. Sometimes when I do this, praying two, three or more times, the person is totally healed. Once I was teaching on healing in church and at the end I asked if there was someone who needed healing who might come forward, so we could put into practice what we were learning. A woman in her late twenties who was in church for the first time raised her hand and came to the front. We briefly heard her story and she said that she'd damaged a tendon while running the day before and that it was very sore. I thanked her for coming forward, and got a few people to pray with her. I gave some gentle guidance, talking through what was going on, as they were praying. After a couple of minutes she tested it out and was very excited, saying it was about 50% better. She was going to sit down, but I asked if she'd like more. She said 'yes'. So the team prayed and this time it was 70% better. They then prayed some more. This time it was 90% improved. They kept going and after a few minutes it was totally healed. She was elated – and needless to say she was back in church the following week! I'm sure she was pleased we didn't stop after the first prayer. This reminds me to keep pursuing God's kingdom.[13]

Seeking the kingdom is what the apostle Paul did until his dying day.[14] He knew from the parables of Jesus that the kingdom is growing, not declining. Isaiah 9:7 tells us just this, declaring: 'Of the increase of his government and peace there will be no end' (NIV 1984). This shows us that God's kingdom is constantly expanding. Our role as disciples is to live in that kingdom, proclaim it and demonstrate it, and see as many lives changed as we can until Christ takes us home to the fullness of the kingdom in heaven.[15]

What a task! What a commission! What a privilege it is to be disciples of God's kingdom.

ACTION: Think about a place in the world which particularly needs the kingdom of God to break in – bringing life, hope, forgiveness, healing and love. Now think about a situation much closer to home (maybe at work or in your family) that would benefit from the kingdom of God coming. Write down each situation and what it might look like for God's kingdom to come.

PRAYER: Now turn both these situations into prayer, praying that God's kingdom would come on earth as in heaven. Ask the Lord to use you in any practical way he desires to see these prayers answered. Then ask him to open your eyes to see more of the kingdom in these coming days, so you can join in with his wonderful work in the world today.

L is for Love

'All you need is love' sang the Beatles, and in many ways they were right! Pure, unadulterated love is the most beautiful thing in the world. So **L is for Love**. But how do you get it? And where does it come from?

The Bible says that God is love.[1] And love comes from him.[2] This means that love is not merely a quality God possesses but is at the heart of his very nature. Our Father is love (see **A is for Abba**). To know God is to know love. To enter the rule and reign of his kingdom is to enter the realm of love. When people experience the kingdom of God (see **K is for Kingdom**) it's normal for them to experience love.[3] St Michael le Belfrey Church, where I am vicar, is in the very centre of the city of York and we often get tourists wandering in to our services as we're worshipping. Sometimes they stay and often they'll ask, 'What is this place? What's going on? I can feel the love.' They're sensing the presence of Jesus and his kingdom – the presence of love.

When the God of love came to earth in Jesus Christ, he came in love.[4] He deeply loved people. With a strong, healing, pure and perfect love. This love drove out fear[5] and brought joy and hope.[6] Tom Wright says that the story of Jesus is 'the story of the love of God, doing for us what we could not do for ourselves'. This story, Wright says, 'produces, again and again, a sense of astonished gratitude'.[7] By his Spirit, the God of love gives his love to his people. It's beautiful to behold. Most of those we baptize at The Belfrey talk of experiencing God's love as central to their conversion.

Followers of Jesus are called to love, like Christ.[8] We're to love all people, even our enemies.[9] We will not do this perfectly but we most certainly can love. We can learn to love. And grow in love.[10] Everything we do must be done in love.[11] And we can persevere in love.[12]

Love is not just being nice. It's about forgiving wrong.[13] Sometimes it involves confrontation, warning, and standing up to abuse and injustice rather than allowing it to continue.[14] If someone we love is about to do something dangerous we should tell them. That is love. A tough, sacrificial kind of love.[15]

Love is more than a feeling. It has to be practically expressed.[16] Anything other than that is just an emotion. According to the Bible, love is an action. It's often evidenced in a selfless choice. In a kind word. In a caring decision. In a giving act.

I know that I, and the church I lead, have much to learn about love, but nevertheless I'm moved time and time again when I see practical examples of love in our church. When I see women and men care for neighbours in need; feed the homeless; visit the housebound and sick; pray for those who are struggling; give to those who are finding it hard to make ends meet. Such acts of love are an inspiration.

Love is best described in 1 Corinthians 13:4–8. This is a great poem or hymn of the early church that the apostle Paul includes in one of his letters. It tells us this about love:

Love is patient, love is kind. It does not envy, it does not boast, it is not proud. It does not dishonour others, it is not self-seeking, it is not easily angered, it keeps no record of wrongs. Love does not delight in evil but rejoices with the truth. It always protects, always trusts, always hopes, always perseveres. Love never fails.

This is how Jesus loves us (see **J is for Jesus**). This is why he died on the cross for us. Because of love.[17]

Re-read the words from 1 Corinthians 13 but this time replace the word 'love' with 'Jesus'. Do you see how loving he is? Do you see how much he loves you? If you've not yet decided to follow Jesus, then maybe now is the time to make that decision. Respond to the love of Jesus by giving yourself to him. As you do that, open your heart to his love and let it flow in. It will, bringing forgiveness, peace and new life. Because Jesus is love.

The way Jesus loves us is how we're supposed to love others. So now re-read the 1 Corinthians 13 passage a third time, but this time replace the word 'love' with your own name. Now you will see that you personally are called to love. Love, however, is not just something you're called to *do*; it's who you *are*. The Lord wants love to be at the centre of every disciple's identity (see **I is for Identity**), because it's at the centre of his. All Christ-followers are to be people of love. The Great Commandment of Jesus says just this: love God and love others.[18] This is how disciples change the world. Not, in the end, through strategies and plans and processes – important as they are. The most important thing is love.

'And now these three remain: faith, hope and love. But the greatest of these is love' (1 Corinthians 13:13).

L is for Love

ACTION: If you've not already read and re-read 1 Corinthians 13, in the way suggested above, do so now. In your journal or notebook, make two columns. In the left-hand column list people you love. In the right-hand column list a few people who you find it hard to love. Resolve to love all these people – in both columns.

PRAYER: Ask the Holy Spirit to show you what you could do to show love to each of the people listed in both columns, in the next few days. It could be sending a note, giving a small gift, making time to be with them, finding a way to encourage them or offering to help in some way. If someone is hard to love because they have wronged you, make a conscious choice to forgive them, rather than waiting for them to say sorry. If a practical idea comes to mind, write it down next to their name. Then pray for the ability and courage to do it so your love is turned from a thought to action.

$\boxed{\text{M}}$ is for Mission

As well as leaving a Great Commandment, Jesus also left his disciples with a Great Commission:

> As you are going, make disciples of all people-groups, baptizing them in the name of the Father and of the Son and of the Holy Spirit, and teaching them everything I have commanded you.[1]

These are Jesus' last orders to his closest followers. It's a call to disciples to be a 'going' people – a people on the move, making more disciples. It's a call for all future disciples to do the same. It's a call to mission. That's why **M is for Mission**.

The reason I am a disciple today is that someone told me about Jesus. In fact it was a number of people. Starting with my parents and grandparents. But I also remember hearing Dick Saunders, a travelling evangelist, tell me that if I believed in Jesus I would receive everlasting life. I also remember Mr Maconochie, a teacher at my school, who encouraged me to follow, and to keep following Jesus. All these people, and others too, didn't keep the message of Christ to themselves but shared it. They took seriously the call to mission. As a result I, and many others, are following Christ today.

Throughout the Bible we read of women and men called by God to 'go'.[2] They're commissioned for mission. In fact the church itself was born in mission for mission (see **C is for**

Church). That's why mission is so central to the make-up of all true disciples. The theologian Emil Brunner expressed it like this: 'the church exists by mission, as fire exists by burning.'[3]

Disciples get their motivation for this mission from God himself.[4] Our Father is the God of mission. Reaching out to a world in love and compassion. He has a mission and he calls us to join in.[5] Church leader Steve Addison summarizes this well when he says: 'Jesus did not come to found a religious organisation. He came to found a missionary movement that would spread to the end of the earth.'[6]

Mission is not something we're to do every now and then. It's more who we are. Disciples are a people on mission. Missional people. A people empowered by the Holy Spirit with a message of love (see **L is for Love**). It's the same message Jesus proclaimed and lived – the good-news message of the kingdom of God[7] (see **K is for Kingdom**). Jesus often called this 'the gospel' – which simply means 'good news'.[8] Proclaiming this gospel message is sometimes called *evangelism*. Evangelism is a crucial aspect of mission that all disciples are called to.

The best way for us to be evangelistic – to be missional through our *words* – is to tell our story. Every disciple has a story of how they discovered the love of our good Father and how they continue to be astounded by his presence and power. Disciples are often asked why they follow Jesus, and telling our stories like this is powerful and changes lives.[9]

While every disciple is called to evangelize, some are especially gifted at it. The Bible calls them 'evangelists'.[10] Evangelists can't stop telling people about Jesus and are good at helping people come to faith. Paul Myers is like this and is part of the staff team at The Belfrey. Paul often tells the story of how Christ has changed his life. Having lived a life of seeking money and fame and finding no satisfaction, and after a number of broken marriages, he found himself addicted to alcohol and ready to end his life. But as he read a Gideon Bible in a hotel room and cried out to a God who he wasn't even sure he believed in, he had an encounter with Christ that gave him hope and began to transform him. He began coming to church and heard the story of the love and care of a good Father and as a result committed the rest of his life to following Jesus Christ and telling others. Paul's life has been transformed by Jesus and he is passionate about passing on the good news. Like so many, Paul has a wonderful story of grace.

The best way for us to be missional through our *actions* is to do something practical to show God's love whenever and wherever we can.[11] Heidi Baker, who works among some of the poorest people in the world, in Mozambique, expresses it like this: 'Love the one in front of you.'[12] This aspect of mission is sometimes called *social action* and, like evangelism, is also an important aspect of mission. Social action can be expressed in simple ways, often by caring for those who are poor and disregarded (see **U is for Underprivileged**). My mother does this very well, not only by giving financially to charities helping the poor but also in the way she particularly goes out of her way to talk with people and thank those who do what are seen as menial jobs, like toilet attendants. Whenever we buy a cup of tea for a homeless person, help clean graffiti off a wall or support a local charity, we're engaging in social action. Often local churches have a few social action projects they particularly lead, ones that make a real difference in their locality. In the UK the collective effect of these social action projects is massive and often underestimated. They're all part of being missional and showing the kingdom of God in practical ways.

For the disciple, both aspects of mission – evangelism and social action – are important. One is no better or more spiritual than the other. Some find one easier than the other and may well have an emphasis in one rather than the other, but nevertheless disciples are called to be engaged in both.[13] To show and tell the good news of Jesus.

Those who want to silence the Christian faith will say that following Jesus is meant to be a private thing. They might possibly welcome our social action but not our evangelism. While of course it's not appropriate for a follower of Christ to force his or her faith on others or share it insensitively, it's incorrect to say that being a disciple is a private matter. Indeed Jesus fundamentally contradicts such a statement.[14] Our faith is public. When we start following Christ we mark it in a public declaration at baptism. The faith is then to be worked out not just in our private lives but in the public sphere of family, community, workplace and world. In fact many great advances and social justice changes have come to the world through disciples doing just this.[15] Christianity was never meant to be private, but public. Disciples are called to change the world.

In recent years the idea of *seven mountains of influence* has helped many disciples identify a sphere of influence where they can be missional and impact the world around them. These seven mountains of influence are: arts and entertainment; business; education; family life; government; media; and religion. Most disciples are called to live or work in at least one of these areas. As we take up the call to be disciples on mission, so each one of us can play our part in helping transform culture and seeing the kingdom of God come on earth as in heaven. As we do this, we look forward to the day when we meet Christ face to face in eternity and hear him say to us: 'Well done, good and faithful servant!'[16]

ACTION: Think about any individuals who have shown you and told you of the love of Christ – and write their names down. Then write down the names of five people who you would love to see become disciples of Jesus.

PRAYER: Give thanks to God for those who have helped you follow Jesus. Then begin to cry out to God in prayer for those five people who you'd love to become disciples. Why not do something practical to help you remember to pray for them – like tie five knots in a piece of leather and fasten it round your wrist? Ask the Lord to use you and others in helping these five people become disciples. Now pray for your church, that it would be a church that takes mission seriously and reaches out boldly and bravely with his love.

N is for New

The Christian faith has been around for two thousand years, so some people think it's old and has little contemporary relevance. With its ancient historic buildings, its clergy often wearing old-fashioned robes, and its liturgy (words of worship) sometimes using medieval language, it's possible to see it as a faith *of* the past *for* the past. But the Bible presents a different picture. It says very little about the 'old' and much more about the 'new' – with God the Father calling all people to find new birth in Christ[1] and declaring 'I am making everything new!'[2] The kingdom of God in which disciples live is dynamic and full of life, constantly restoring and reviving.[3] This renewing work of God is exciting and energizing and central to the life of discipleship.[4] That's why **N is for New**.

God likes the new. That doesn't mean he or his followers should dislike the old. Living in the historic city of York, I appreciate its rich history and fascinating traditions. People have been baptizing and worshipping on or near the site of St Michael le Belfrey Church since the early seventh century. That's an amazing heritage! We must honour the past, and the Bible says it's really important to not forget what the Lord has done.[5] But at The Belfrey we want to not just love our history but to be making history! We want to innovate and be creative. After all, God is the great Creator.[6] He is an artist.[7] An architect.[8] A pioneer.[9] So in our witness we're seeking to bring new life.[10] In our worship and communication we're looking to create new sounds, songs and images.[11] We love to tell the new stories of God at work[12] and to show and tell the (old) good-news story in new, creative ways.[13]

For the disciple, the new begins at baptism (see **S is for Sacraments**) – where a disciple becomes 'a new creation', because 'the old has gone; the new has come'[14] as he or she embraces a new identity, given by our good Father in Jesus Christ (see **I is for Identity**). Every time someone becomes a Christian this is a work of new life.[15] The indwelling Spirit then continues to re-new us, growing his fruit of character in our lives,[16] bringing new thinking on many issues,[17] and transforming our attitudes and actions so we become more and more Christ-like.[18] This is a lifetime's work which continues to our dying day, as God brings the new to us, preparing us for eternity.[19]

I am constantly amazed how, having read the Bible many times, I still discover new things as I read. The Spirit of God loves to speak and show me things, applying the old word in a new way. This is true corporately in our families and churches and communities. The God of the new always has more to say and show and bring. God loves to bring restoration and regeneration which is often expressed in our communities in new innovative projects, new businesses, new parks and leisure spaces, new housing projects and even brand-new cities!

Heaven – the 'Holy City'[20] and final destiny for disciples – is described in the Bible as 'a new heaven and a new earth'[21] which means that everything will be renewed – including ourselves. We'll be given new bodies[22] that will never grow tired or weary. We will be given new assignments.[23] New homes.[24]

A brand-new life.[25] It'll be creative and beautiful and rich and perfect. The best is yet to come!

Until that day the Spirit of God will continue to bring the new, here on earth. New thoughts. New language. New love. New seasons.[26] As these new things come not just to individuals but also to communities, regions and nations,[27] so these new movements of his Spirit often touch particular people-groups,[28] and with these movements particular emphases are renewed in the church and society.

As we look back at history, we see that God brings new cultural movements which influence wider society. This includes new theological, philosophical, artistic and cultural emphases that express the kingdom of God. Often this occurs as part of or after a renewing move of the Spirit which comes first to the church.[29] The church sees a great increase in people becoming disciples, with miraculous signs and wonders following.[30] These transformed individuals and churches then bring transformation to the wider society, impacting culture.

While disciples celebrate and welcome God's Spirit bringing the new, not every new emphasis in church or wider society will necessarily be good or inspired by God. Wise consideration is needed. For disciples the Bible is always the primary standard for such evaluation.[31] *Sola Scriptura* ('Scripture Alone') has been the rallying cry of many past disciples who've wanted to ensure that change in church and society is change for the good. However, having listened to God in Scripture, it's good for Christ-followers to use the rich resources of *reason* (thinking something through), *tradition* (studying the wisdom of the past) and *experience* (seeing what God is doing today) as secondary means of discernment.[32] These enable us to see, appreciate and enjoy what is genuinely a new work of God's Spirit.

I recently enjoyed climbing a mountain in Yosemite National Park in California with my eldest son, Ben. The climb took a long time and I was exhausted when I reached the top. But before we began we chose to appreciate the journey. The hike was tough but beautiful and we stopped many times to look at things like the trees, the flowers, the eagles and lizards and deer. We savoured the spectacular views and enjoyed what we were discovering. That made the final destination even more rewarding. Similarly there's much to see and discover about the new life in the kingdom of God on planet earth. Then when our life here is done, we don't just die and that's the end.[33] Neither are we reincarnated.[34] Instead disciples are assured of new life in all its fullness, beyond the grave in heaven.[35] Christ won this marvellous future for us through his death and resurrection, saving us from a destiny separated from God in hell,[36] and it's the most fantastic gift![37] However, disciples mustn't get so caught up in this future destination that we miss the joy of the journey. We're called to live not just for the future but in the present, and cherish each moment as a new opportunity of grace.

God is renewing the earth. Renewing his church. Renewing individuals. In anticipation for the final day when all things will be made new in heaven. This means disciples need never be bored nor get dispirited. There's always more. Always new things to enjoy and discover. The best is yet to come! This is the wonder of being a disciple of Jesus Christ.

ACTION: What new things have you been discovering recently about life and about being a disciple? Write them down. Think about the place where you spend most time in the day – perhaps your workplace, school or university, or home. Is there something new and fresh you feel inspired to encourage and bring? Write it down.

PRAYER: Say sorry to the Lord for when you've not been open to the new things that God is doing and you've chosen the known and the familiar for the sake of an easy life. Thank him that he's the God of new creation. Ask for the help of his Spirit today to be part of something new he is doing, offering him the things you've written down today.

O is for Obedience

I was sitting alone in a café on a warm summer's day last year, enjoying a good book and a refreshing glass of sparkling juice. I'd picked up the juice bottle from the counter, noticing it contained lemon, elderflower and tarragon, but I'd not taken any further notice of what was written on it. As I reached to pour more of the juice from the bottle into my glass, I glimpsed the label and was stopped short by what I saw. It said 'Sparkling Obedience'. The phrase arrested me: 'Sparkling Obedience.' In that moment it felt as if God was speaking to me, reminding me that obedient people sparkle. Rather than seeing obedience as a negative aspect of discipleship, I was seeing how, like a glistening diamond which catches the eye, obedience is attractive. Like a cool carbonated drink that quenches a parched mouth, obedient disciples bring refreshment. Living obediently is good, inviting and satisfying. I looked again at the label and this time couldn't see the word 'Obedience'. It actually said 'Sparkling Organics' and I'd obviously misread it! But it was too late. The Lord had got my attention. Obedient people are meant to sparkle. Paul Harcourt, National Leader of the New Wine movement in the UK, agrees, recognizing that the motivation for obedience is much more than self-restraint, saying that 'choosing to obey God is always choosing the better thing'.[1] The Bible similarly agrees. That's why **O is for Obedience**.

Some disciples live obediently out of duty. While there's some benefit in this,[2] our Heavenly Father wants the main motivation for obedience to be love.[3] Christ has done everything for us, so in response we want to please and honour him.[4] As disciples do this more and more, they realize that living obediently is actually the best way to live.

God wants us to learn obedience from childhood[5] by obeying our parents (while parents need to make sure that what they ask of their children is reasonable and they don't 'exasperate' them![6]). We need to obey our church leaders,[7] encouraging them (see **E is for Encourage**), trusting that they're praying for us and assuming their intentions are good. But most of all, we need to obey Christ,[8] God's Living Word, and the Bible, God's written word.[9]

In the Bible, obedience is a primary sign of discipleship. Christ is the Master, not us.[10] He is the King, not us.[11] All authority rests in him, not us.[12] This means that when Jesus speaks to people the appropriate answer is 'Yes, Lord'.[13] David Watson put it very clearly when he said: 'To say, "No Lord" is a contradiction in terms.'[14]

In the New Testament, Simon Peter is the first person to follow Christ.[15] In many ways he is also a model disciple – not because he gets everything right (because he doesn't) but because he's the first disciple and he learns from his mistakes.[16] Peter is a fisherman. One day, before Peter became a Christ-follower and after a night of catching no fish, Jesus asks him to go out fishing again. Peter is reluctant. He's caught nothing all night, is tired and back on shore, has cleaned his nets and is ready to go home.[17] It would've been quite understandable for Peter to say 'no', but instead he says 'Because you say so, Jesus, I will'.[18] That's the attitude of the true disciple. It's the attitude of willing submission that sometimes goes against what by nature we might desire, or what our culture might commend. That's why obedience is one of the marks, if not the first mark, of discipleship.

If human beings want to become good at something, then learning obedience and discipline is crucial. Aristotle knew this, saying 'We are what we repeatedly do. Excellence, then, is not an act, but a habit.' Malcolm Gladwell, in his book *Outliers*, points to helpful research showing that those who excel in their field have normally given at least 10,000 hours of their time to it.[19] Gifting is clearly important, but so is steady and consistent discipline. Disciples are 'disciplined ones' (see **D is for Disciplines**). This reminds us that discipline comes from continued obedience.

The Bible has many commands. They're there for our good, and given by our good Father (see **A is for Abba**). They include really helpful things like: 'Tell the truth';[20] 'Be generous';[21] 'Do not steal';[22] 'Flee from sexual immorality';[23] 'Overcome evil with good';[24] 'Do not murder';[25] 'Practise hospitality';[26] 'Pay taxes'.[27] Disciples need to know what the Bible says about these and many other things, and then put them into practice. If we don't read the Bible, we won't know what God thinks about many subjects and won't see the benefits of obedience.

So we must read the Bible. *And* we must also put it into practice. To do that is to be like a wise person who built their house on rock, and when the storms came the house stood firm. But if we only hear but don't respond obediently, Jesus said we're like a foolish person who built their house on sand, and when the storms came their house fell to the ground with a great crash![28]

Over time, living obediently should come more and more naturally to disciples, as the Spirit transforms us and we day by day commit ourselves to being 'a living sacrifice'.[29] Jesus has saved us from sin and death and we're now his servants.[30] That should be enough motivation in itself! However, before he died, Jesus taught his disciples about obedience and gave them new motivation, saying: 'I no longer call you servants . . . Instead, I have called you friends'.[31] We should love him and do what he says because he loves us! We are his friends, and we know that, as our friend, what he says will always be good and helpful.

Since my late teens I've felt God call me to not drink alcohol for the rest of my life. I don't think this is a call for every disciple, but it is for some. That was true for various people in Bible times[32] so it shouldn't surprise us that some today are called to this, and to other disciplines too, either for a limited period of time[33] or for life.[34] I can give other reasons why I don't drink alcohol, but the main one is that I'm wanting to be obedient. I know this is what God wants for me, and I want to serve him, so I'm happy to make this minor sacrifice for the sake of the kingdom of God. I trust that he's a good Father and he knows what's best.[35]

Bill Johnson is right when he says: 'It is in the process of obedience that we gain understanding.'[36] Many disciples want to learn, grow and develop quickly. But the work of maturing as a disciple is slow work. There's no short cut. It starts and continues in obedience. So start now. Today.

ACTION: Take stock of your life at present. What things are you doing at the moment that are acts of obedience to the Lord? Write them down. If your list is short, what does that mean? Is there something in particular you sense the Lord asking you to do at present? Write it down.

PRAYER: Look at the things you have written down and ask the Lord to fill you with his Spirit so that you may live an increasingly obedient life – out of joy rather than just duty. Pray for another disciple you know who is struggling to live obediently to God's word in a particular area of their life.

P is for Prayer

You don't have to be a follower of Jesus very long before realizing that nothing of lasting significance happens without prayer. That's why **P is for Prayer**.

Prayer is one of the main distinguishing features of disciples. We are a praying people. It's what we do. When Jesus gives basic teaching on discipleship in Matthew 6, he highlights three foundational disciplines he expects his disciples to practise: giving[1] (see **G is for Giving**), fasting[2] (see **D is for Disciplines**), and praying.[3] All three are full of exponential potential, releasing spiritual power greater than the human effort put in.

I met a man at a conference recently who told me that he'd suffered from varying degrees of anxiety and hadn't slept well or through the night for many years. Part of my prayer for him was that he'd sleep deeply that night and right through to the morning. I saw him the very next day and asked how he'd slept. With a big smile on his face he said, 'Like a baby! It was wonderful!' Such is the power of prayer – and all disciples are called to join in!

Prayer is communication with our Heavenly Father. It's talking to him and with him, and listening to him. It's basic to discipleship. In the same way that human relationships are sustained and flourish by good communication, so a disciple's relationship with God is nourished and deepened as he or she talks with him in prayer.

Jesus is our role model for prayer. For the last two thousand years, disciples have loved reading the four gospel accounts of Jesus' life and discovering wonderful things about prayer from their Master. Like his first followers we learn from him. A good prayer for disciples to pray is: 'Lord, teach us to pray'.[4] A good prayer for disciples to learn is the Lord's Prayer, which can be prayed in one go, or broken down into small sections and used as a springboard to further prayer. Greg Downes at The Belfrey sometimes teaches on the Lord's Prayer from Matthew 6:9–13, using the acronym 'PRAY' – helpfully encouraging us to **P**raise (v. 9), **R**epent (vv. 12–13), **A**sk (v. 11) and **Y**ield (v. 10).

When we talk with God it's less important that we use the right words and more important that we share our hearts.[5] In the same way that a lover is not looking for polished words but for vulnerable devotion, so God is looking for honesty[6] and reverence.[7] Posture can be helpful – standing with hands raised to heaven[8] (that's how many prayed in the early church), or kneeling, bowing and prostrating oneself on the floor.[9] It's good to pray out loud. (If you don't, you might find it harder praying out loud with others, as you're not used to hearing the sound of your own voice.) But it's good too to pray quietly under your breath or even to pray silently. I journal regularly and lots of my journal entries end up in prayer – as I write down my reflections on life's experiences and then offer them to the Lord. Sometimes I pray 'thank you' prayers. Sometimes 'sorry' prayers. Sometimes 'please' prayers. The most important thing to remember is this: there are lots of ways to pray, so pray!

Not all of my prayers are answered as I expect. Not all of my prayers are answered immediately.[10] But I know that all of my prayers reach the heart of my good Father who loves to hear my prayers more than I love to pray them. He wants me to talk with him and he wants to talk with me.[11] As Nicky Gumbel says: 'If God answers "Yes", He is increasing your faith. If "Wait", He is increasing your patience. If "No", He has something better for you.'[12]

When we're feeling low we often don't feel like praying, despite it being the best thing we could do. We have an enemy who doesn't want us to pray, who wants to discourage us from praying and who is scared of our prayers. (It's not a coincidence that the main passage in the Bible on spiritual warfare, in Ephesians 6, ends with an encouragement to pray.[13]) So pray, even in hard times.

I was taught by my father to begin every day with reading the Bible and prayer.[14] After many years I still do that. It's been one of the best pieces of advice of my whole life and it's sustained my relationship with the Lord. I also try to pray with others as much as possible. Jesus said that power is released when you get together with two or three people and pray.[15] What were the disciples doing after Jesus ascended and before the Spirit came in power and was poured out? The answer is: they were praying![16] Since then, every new and reviving move of God has begun in prayer and been sustained in prayer. As the nineteenth-century evangelist D.L. Moody said: 'Every move of God can be traced to a kneeling figure.'[17] That's why at The Belfrey we've established St Cuthbert's House of Prayer, a community of people praying and seeking God for his transformation of the north of England. St Cuthbert was known as 'the apostle to the North' and we believe it's no coincidence that the Lord has provided a prayerful space, named after the apostle to the North, in which to cry out in prayer for revival in the North in our day.

As well as taking time to pray each day, disciples need to remain prayerful throughout the day. The more we do this, the more we become increasingly aware of the presence of God with us, and we regularly offer up prayers to him and learn to walk in the Spirit.[18] This is what the Bible means when it says 'Pray continually'.[19]

It's corny, but true, that 'seven days without prayer makes one weak'! So pray. You won't be disappointed.

ACTION: Write down the words 'Thank you' and list ten things for which you are thankful. Then write the word 'Sorry' and write down anything you need to say sorry about. Finally write the word 'Please' and write down five things you'd like to ask God for.

PRAYER: Now turn all these things into prayer and talk to God about them. Tell him honestly about them and other matters that are on your heart today too. He longs to hear from you and to talk with you about them. If you sense him communicating with you, write it down. Then worship him, telling him how wonderful he is. Allow time for his Spirit to rest on you, and enjoy his presence.

Q is for Quarrel

Disciples fall out. We are humans and so from time to time get cross, frustrated and hurt. It happens to me, and to us at The Belfrey. Jesus knew this and so left us with some of the clearest, simplest and most helpful teaching in the world on this. In my experience many Christ-followers in the West fail to put this teaching into practice when they feel wronged, somehow feeling that it doesn't apply to them. But it does. It's for us all. Every disciple needs to put Jesus' teaching on quarrelling into practice! So **Q is for Quarrel**.

So how should we handle conflict? What should we do? Christ teaches a four-stage process, found in Matthew 18:15–20:

[15]If your brother or sister sins, go and point out their fault, just between the two of you. If they listen to you, you have won them over. [16]But if they will not listen, take one or two others along, so that 'every matter may be established by the testimony of two or three witnesses.' [17]If they still refuse to listen, tell it to the church; and if they refuse to listen even to the church, treat them as you would a pagan or a tax collector.

[18]Truly I tell you, whatever you bind on earth will be bound in heaven, and whatever you loose on earth will be loosed in heaven.

[19]Again, truly I tell you that if two of you on earth agree about anything they ask for, it will be done for them by my Father in heaven. [20]For where two or three gather in my name, there am I with them.

Step 1: one to one (18:15a: if someone sins against you . . .)

Something happens. You feel hurt. What should you do? Go alone and see the person responsible and say 'This has happened. This is how I feel.' (It's best not to go in all guns blazing and say: 'Look what you've done . . .!')

This is not easy, but it's important. I remember as a fairly new disciple reading these words of Jesus and as a result going to someone who I felt had treated me badly. I'd forgiven him but couldn't shake it off and found that it was spoiling our relationship. When I explained how I felt, he said he didn't realize the effect of what he'd done and was quick to apologize. We talked and prayed and all was well. It showed me that this teaching of Jesus really works!

So don't talk to others.[1] Go straight to the person. In fact, if someone comes gossiping to you about what so-and-so has done, you should ask if they've been to see the person first. If not, politely but firmly end the conversation by telling them to go and talk with them face to face. As Nicky Gumbel says: 'A lot of problems in the world would be solved if we talked to each other instead of about each other.'[2]

When someone has hurt them, most people do the opposite of what Jesus teaches here. They tell everyone except the person in question. Occasionally I've discovered I've unknowingly offended someone but I'm the last person to find out! That is frustrating. If disciples did what Jesus said here, there'd be a lot sorted out behind closed doors. Gossip would decrease and the church would be a much healthier community. We'd be stronger and more united (see **C is for Church**).

Jesus says: 'If they listen to you, you have won them over.' So this is the hope of the one to one: reconciliation and restoration. Because reconciliation is something God loves.[3]

So one to one is always the first step. But what if the other person doesn't accept what you say?

Step 2: two or three (v. 16)

Go again – but this time take 'two or three witnesses' (other disciples). Present your case, let them respond and maybe let the witnesses ask a few questions of you both. The hope is still reconciliation and restoration. Very often that happens after a one to one, but if they won't listen to you, don't give up. Try again, but this time you need to discreetly tell one or two others in confidence and then go together to the person with whom you have the issue. This is step 2.

But what if they still don't accept what you're saying and apologize?

Step 3: tell the church (v. 17a)

'The church' here could mean 'the whole church' (i.e. you need to gather a whole church meeting) or it could mean 'the leadership of the church' (those who represent the whole church on a day-to-day basis). My recommendation would be to go to the leadership, as it reduces the potential for gossip.

It's very important that you go through step 1 and step 2 before you do this third step. Follow the steps Jesus gives, in the order Jesus instructs. We don't go to leadership or someone 'above' the person first. This is a good principle in all contexts – including workplaces as well as churches.

Most church leaders know what it's like to have someone approach them complaining about somebody else in church. When someone comes to me like this, I normally ask if they've first spoken to the person directly. Often they haven't, so I tell them to do what Jesus tells us here – to go through step 1 and step 2 before getting to step 3. It's the best and most honouring way to handle things. I know what it is to be on the receiving end of complaints about me given straight to my superiors by people who've not been through steps 1 and 2. It's disempowering and disrespectful. Every time, I wish they had come to talk with me first, as Jesus says.

But what if the other person doesn't accept the view of 'the church'?

Step 4: they leave the church (v. 17b)

If we reach this point, Jesus says we should regard the person as someone 'outside'. That means the leadership regretfully ask them to leave the church.[4] It doesn't mean we treat them badly, but with respect, dignity, love and prayer, like Jesus treated those outside the church.

So this is the very simple and effective process Jesus teaches for disciples to practise when they find themselves in a quarrel. It's about doing confrontation without being confrontational. And it works well. I've not always got this right in the past. Sometimes I've not confronted someone when I should. But when I have, it's always been helpful, if not easy. It stops things festering.

Here are three final thoughts on quarrelling.

1. The least effective (but easiest) way to handle conflict is either to push it under the carpet or to walk away from the relationship. Pushing an issue under the carpet never works. It has a way of crawling out again. We must not put it off, but deal with it.[5] Walking away – although often appealing – is actually the cowardly thing to do. That's *not* the attitude of Jesus Christ. He calls us to be brave: to face up to conflict and work for relationships to be restored.[6]

2. If we don't follow this process, what happens? The answer is that gossip spreads and rumours circulate. But there should be no place for that in God's church.[7] If we handle things badly, we make room for the devil to come in – and he will – seeking to destroy, not build; to tear down, not build up.[8] In fact sometimes we can end up doing the devil's work for him as we allow groups or cliques to form around particular issues or personalities. This can be a bad witness to those outside church.

3. If someone comes to you and says you've offended them, then what? Listen to them. If you know you've acted badly then say so and apologize. If you don't think you've done anything wrong, don't take offence. Have a tough skin. Be humble and say something like: 'If I've offended you, I'm sorry. If I've done something without realizing, I'm sorry.'[9] Then pray together, because when disciples pray, the presence of God comes, bringing forgiveness, healing and love.

Finally, when it comes to conflict, never forget: God's given us two ears and one mouth – and we're to use them in that proportion![10]

ACTION: Is there someone who has hurt or offended you, who you need to be reconciled with? If so, go through the stages listed above, starting with step 1: going to see them one to one. Don't wait for them to contact you. It might never happen. Be brave and make contact today and fix a time to meet for the purpose of forgiveness and reconciliation.

PRAYER: Pray for all your relationships, that they'd be healthy and good. Pray for someone close to you who has fallen out with someone. Pray for reconciliation. Pray that you would have wisdom to help them go through the steps Jesus outlines in Matthew 18 so things can be right again.

R is for Repentance

Repentance means change. A change of direction. It's someone deciding to change their mind and go a different way. There's much repentance required if we're to follow Jesus, grow in discipleship and make the difference in the world which God desires. This means that repentance is good. It's good for us and good for others and originates in our good Father. That's why **R is for Repentance**.

To begin following Jesus requires repentance and faith (see **F is for Faith**).[1] We see something attractive about Jesus and his kingdom (see **K is for Kingdom**) and turn around to follow him. In fact, when we see Jesus at work and his kingdom impacting the life of people round us, repentance is the right and natural response. That's why, whenever the kingdom of God is announced and proclaimed, people are invited to repent and change.[2]

Repentance is sometimes associated with feeling bad about something we've done wrong. That actually isn't repentance – that's feeling remorse – and is often how we feel when our consciences are convicted by the Holy Spirit. To repent requires more. It requires action. A change of mind and direction. Going down a different path.[3] Our good Father loves repentance. He sent Jesus to die for our repentance and through his Spirit calls us to a life of repentance. It's all a response to his great love and kindness.[4]

On many occasions the Lord has convinced me of my sin, and I've had to repent. Occasionally it's been a struggle, as I've had to reluctantly acknowledge my wayward heart. But most of the time when the Spirit shines light on dirt in my life and my sin is clearly exposed, I've found it best to simply say, 'Yes, Lord, you're right. That was wrong. I am sorry. I turn away from that.' If it's possible to put a plan of action in place to stop me doing it again, I will then do that.

I'm in a long-standing prayer triplet with two close friends and sometimes we confess our sins to each other, and ask the Lord to help us to repent.[5] This keeps me accountable and can be humbling and powerful.

On lots of occasions I've sat with people as they've repented – maybe for the very first time as they come to Christ, or in response to a particular issue in their life. Every time, it is a profound privilege as people vow to change and ask for the fruit of repentance to be seen in their lives.

Jesus told a beautiful story of repentance, often called 'The Prodigal Son'.[6] It's a story of a young man who leaves his father's home and squanders his inheritance on parties and prostitutes. One day, when his money has run out, he comes to his senses and decides to turn around and go home. It's a wonderful picture of repentance. He returns to his father, sorrowful for his selfish actions, asking to be no longer a son in the household but a slave. But the father, rather than being angry, is overjoyed to see his long-lost son. He forgives him. Reinstates him. And gives him all the benefits of being in his family. It's a story of deep grace – of the good Father's forgiving and giving love. And of the repentance of a human being from a life of selfishness and sin.

But repenting isn't just about turning from sin. Sometimes it's simply choosing to go a different way, not because the old way was wrong but because it's time for something new (see **N is for New**). In those circumstances it's not that we've been doing anything wrong; it's just time for change. That's why the Bible even occasionally talks of God repenting.[7] This means that the life of discipleship is about constant repentance. As we grow and develop and change and mature, disciples should be repenting all the time. Sometimes this will involve saying sorry and putting things right; at other times it will involve adjusting our thinking and as a result changing our behaviour, as our minds are renewed and transformed (see **N is for New**).[8]

Jesus gave a simple picture to the first disciples to describe this life of repentance. It was the picture of pruning.[9] I enjoy gardening and like pruning shrubs and bushes. Some require a lot of pruning and the immediate effect can be quite shocking, so much so that my wife Sam sometimes asks, 'Have you killed it?!' Jesus said that in the same way that a vine grows and then, to be productive in the future, requires pruning, so do we. But at times it can look and feel painful and difficult. But God knows best and will cut things back in our lives for the sake of fruitfulness.[10] Some of these things, no doubt, will be bad things. But some will not be wrong in themselves; it's just time for them to go, to make room for future growth.

In our individualistic culture it's easy to think of repentance as just a personal thing, but there are many examples in the Bible of corporate repentance. Families can change direction.[11] Churches can too.[12] So can towns and cities.[13] Even whole nations.[14] This means that repentance is a lifestyle that all people are called to.

'Change' is at the heart of the message of God. To a world lost and lacking direction, God says: 'Change your mind. Change your direction. Change your life.' This is God's call, because he loves us with an incredible love. He wants none to perish. He wants all to repent.[15]

ACTION: Ask yourself: what do I make of this idea that following Jesus is a life of constant repentance? Have I begun to do this? Is there something that God is asking me to turn away from today? Or a new positive task or project or direction he's drawing me to?

PRAYER: Turn all these things to prayer. Give them to God. Ask for his help, particularly if there's an area of your life that you know you need to turn from, but you find it really hard to do so. Thank God that he has good plans for you. And for your loved ones. Pray that you will model good repentance to those around you.

$\boxed{\text{S}}$ is for Sacraments

A 'sacrament' is an outward sign of an inward reality. The two most important sacraments in the New Testament are baptism and Holy Communion. Baptism marks the way in. Holy Communion marks the way on. Both are important. That's why **S is for Sacraments**.

The Bible word 'baptism' comes from a Greek word which means 'immersion'. Baptism is about being immersed in God and it's normally expressed symbolically by immersion in water (or being sprinkled if you're not able to go under water).[1] The amount of water isn't particularly important, which means that you're not less baptized if less water is used! However, the picture is one of being drenched in God – which is why at The Belfrey we encourage full immersion, if possible.

Baptism marks a change in identity for the follower of Jesus (see **I is for Identity**). The old has gone and the new has come.[2] As church leaders Fred and Sharon Wright say: 'Baptizing is not just getting people wet, but getting them transformed with new identity.'[3] That's why disciples are baptized people. In fact baptism is the main sign of being a follower of Jesus and belonging to him and his church.

A number of years ago I met a girl called Sam. We became friends and the more I got to know her, the more I thought she was wonderful. We began dating and I soon realized I was smitten and wanted to spend the rest of my life loving her and so I asked her to marry me – and she agreed! So we got married.

On 18 August 1990. Our marriage was the public sign that this relationship was for life. Now, all these years later, we're still married and very pleased we are. Similarly, as we get to know Jesus Christ we come to a point when we realize that this is a relationship of love and is *for life*. Once we know that and want to commit to that, we should be baptized.

Sometimes people delay baptism, thinking they need to know lots more about Jesus and the Christian faith first. But that's not right. I certainly didn't know everything about Sam before we were married. I simply knew enough to be able to say that the relationship was for life. And it's the same with Christ. We need to know enough to be able to say with integrity that it's a relationship till death do us part.[4] Then we spend a lifetime discovering how truly amazing he is!

The Bible knows nothing of an unbaptized believer.[5] It's not right – it's like cohabiting without marrying. Neither is baptism something just for mature believers. Rather baptism is the first step for someone who has decided to follow Christ.[6] So while it's great to begin praying and reading the Bible, and also good to make a conscious choice to follow Jesus, the main way the Bible says we show commitment to the life of discipleship is through baptism. Christ is committed to us and we now commit to him. For life. In baptism.

Baptism signifies repentance – a change of direction (see **R is for Repentance**). Believers identify with the death and resurrection of Jesus.[7] In going under the water they bury everything from the past that's wrong and in coming up out of the water they welcome the new resurrection life that Jesus has won.[8] When we think of baptism we often think of the ceremony (sometimes called a 'rite') where we publicly get wet, but it's actually much more than the one-off event. It's a life decision that needs to be lived out day by day as we continue to immerse ourselves in Christ and his Spirit.[9] This immersed life is a life given over in love and service to Christ. It's a life offered to God in worship (see **W is for Worship**). We now belong to him. We are Jesus people. He is our Lord,[10] our Master,[11] our King.[12] This is the devoted life of the baptized.

If you've decided to follow Jesus and aren't yet baptized, then you should be! It's your next step. Obviously if you're not sure you're ready to make a life commitment to Christ, then wait. But as soon as you're ready, get baptized. Christ is certainly ready for you and fully committed to you.[13] He showed that in dying for you on the cross.[14] He wants to live in relationship with you, every day. His hands are outstretched to you and he invites you to live in a love relationship with him.[15] He will never give up on you and will be faithful to you. Always.[16] So believe and be baptized.[17]

Having been baptized, it's important to continue to live the baptized life – immersed in God and living as 'dead to sin but alive to God in Christ'.[18] In order to keep remembering, marking and sharing this with other disciples, we don't get baptized repeatedly, as baptism is a one-off act done when we first come to Christ. Instead we regularly take Holy Communion.

Holy Communion has various names in different churches. It's sometimes called 'the Lord's Supper' or 'the Eucharist' and it's sometimes called other things too. It's the regular taking of bread and wine to remember all that Jesus has done through his cross and resurrection.

A few years ago I met a young man who'd just decided to follow Jesus. He was serious about his commitment and wanted to grow. He had no church background whatsoever and so we decided to meet regularly to help build some good foundations.

We'd meet every couple of weeks to talk, read the Bible and pray, and we did this for a number of months and it was great to see him grow in his faith. I remember one occasion, fairly early on, when he came to see me, rather troubled. 'I went to church on Sunday,' he said, 'and something really weird was happening.' 'Oh,' I said, 'tell me.' 'They had this mini-meal kind of thing, and we were invited forward and we were told it was about eating Jesus' body and drinking his blood. I wasn't sure about it at all. Was it OK?' I smiled and reassured him it was OK, and we spent some time looking at what the Bible had to say about the death of Jesus and how we were to celebrate it regularly, as he'd done for the first time the previous Sunday. He was reassured – which was good! But that meeting reminded me that to someone brand new to the faith with no church background, the idea behind Holy Communion can seem rather strange. It needs to be explained.

Before Jesus died he gathered his followers and shared bread and wine with them, telling them that the bread stood for 'his body' and the wine for 'his blood'.[19] From the early days of the church, Christians continued to regularly share bread and wine in this way.[20] The Bible teaches that this is not a full meal of bread and wine, but a simple sharing to remember Jesus.[21] Disciples should make sure they're right with God and others before taking Holy Communion.[22] And the church will continue to do this until Christ returns.[23] At Communion, Christ nourishes us and we receive afresh his resurrection life.[24] For many followers of Jesus, receiving Holy Communion is one of the main ways that they're filled with and experience the Holy Spirit.

While Holy Communion is a meal for the baptized and is to be received in faith (see **F is for Faith**), there are many examples in church history of people who are not yet following Jesus but who encounter him through the bread and wine.[25] Recently at The Belfrey a young woman came forward to receive the bread and wine but then stopped, telling my colleague Ben Doolan that she wasn't yet a believer in Christ. Ben talked briefly with her and realized she was ready to be a disciple, so he led her in a prayer of commitment to Jesus there and then. She immediately marked that by sharing the bread and wine – it was the most natural thing to do! She was also baptized at the next opportunity.

Some church services of Holy Communion are very serious and sombre affairs. While it's right to remember Jesus' sacrificial death with reverence and awe, it's something to celebrate and be thankful for. In fact the word 'eucharist', which is the word used for Holy Communion in many churches that value formality in worship, literally means 'celebration'! The death and resurrection of Jesus is something to rejoice in. He died for our liberty, so that we might know the love of our good Father and great joy in our hearts!

So the sign of beginning the journey of faith is baptism, and the sign of continuing is Holy Communion. These two sacraments are basic but important. They unite followers of Jesus in a simple unity in the church, Christ's body. They remind us that we stand in a long line of disciples who over two thousand years have been baptizing and sharing bread and wine, to worship and adore Jesus Christ, who died and rose again, so that we might have life.[26]

ACTION: Write down the date of your baptism and what you remember about it. If you aren't yet baptized but are following Jesus, speak to your local church leader and arrange to talk about baptism soon. Look up some of the references to the bread and wine and remind yourself of what they signify. Are you taking Holy Communion regularly? If not, make sure you're part of a church that regularly celebrates the death and resurrection of Jesus in this way.

PRAYER: Be thankful to your good Father that he sent Jesus to die for you. If you're not yet baptized, pray for an opportunity to experience baptism soon. Pray that as you regularly share bread and wine in church, the Holy Spirit will draw you close to Christ and help you adore him more. Finally, ask the Lord to give you an opportunity to talk about your baptism to a friend, colleague or family member today.

T is for Trinity

My long-standing friend and colleague at The Belfrey, Greg Downes, has two beautiful young daughters – the youngest of whom is called 'Trinity.' Greg and his wife Tamie named her Trinity to reflect the nature of the God they adore – the Trinitarian God of the Bible – the God who's revealed himself to humanity as Father, Son and Holy Spirit. Disciples worship the Trinity – which is why **T is for Trinity**.

The word 'Trinity' comes from the Latin word *trinus* meaning 'threefold'. From it we get words like 'tricycle' (a three-wheel bike), 'triathlon' (a three-event sport) and 'tripod' (a three-legged stand). Since the first century AD, Christians have believed that the one God who we read about in the Bible actually exists in three persons: Father, Son and Holy Spirit. In the third century the Latin theologian Tertullian coined the term 'Trinity', explaining that the Father, Son and Holy Spirit were 'One in essence – but not one in Person'. They are three. Three in One. And One in Three.

The word 'Trinity' is not used in the Bible, but the idea that all three persons are God is seen clearly in Scripture. Here are just three examples.

1. At the baptism of Jesus we see a wonderful interplay between all three persons, with the Son being baptized, the Spirit descending and the Father speaking.[1]

2. The first letter of Peter begins by greeting people 'who have been chosen according to the . . . Father, through the sanctifying work of the Spirit, to be obedient to Jesus Christ'.[2] We see there that Peter and the earliest Christians clearly believed in a Trinitarian God.

3. Paul's second letter to the Corinthians ends with words of Trinitarian blessing (sometimes known as 'the Grace'): 'May the grace of the Lord Jesus Christ, and the love of God, and the fellowship of the Holy Spirit be with you all.'[3]

Some people find the idea of God being Trinity intellectually difficult at first, but they're then helped by observing the created world. A clover has three leaves on one head. And water exists in three different states, as a liquid (water), as a gas (steam) and as a solid (ice), and yet all three are forms of one substance. So the idea of God being One and yet Three is not beyond the realms of human imagination!

As we read the Bible – both New Testament and Old – understanding God as Trinity makes sense of the way he has revealed himself to humanity. Since the early church, followers of Jesus have affirmed this, and there are helpful and rich writings on this, especially in the Roman, Orthodox and Celtic Christian traditions. The church realized that understanding God as Trinity makes best sense of him, so much so that for many years it's been recognized as an important test of orthodoxy (right belief), with all the Christian creeds (statements of faith) affirming God to be Father, Son and Spirit. So if you find yourself in a faith community that denies the Trinity, move on and find a more right-believing church in which to belong.

Recognizing God as Trinity has implications not just for our beliefs but also for our relationships. We observe in the Bible the three persons of the Trinity existing and working in a beautiful love-relationship together.[4] They affirm and encourage and praise each other. They honour each other. They love. As such, the Trinity becomes our model for all human relationships. We love, because God is love.[5]

In some historic churches a creed or statement of faith is recited in every act of worship, as a reminder of what these disciples believe. At The Belfrey we always use a short creed at baptism services and sometimes at other services too. Sometimes we sing creedal songs that declare the truth of what we believe about our great, Trinitarian God. We always end our services by blessing our people and sending them out to impact the world in the name of God who is Father, Son and Holy Spirit. This is the Trinitarian God whom disciples gladly serve.

The most important thing for disciples is not to get too hung up on the Trinity or worry about which Person you're singing or praying to. If it comes from your heart, be assured that God receives it all as worship.[6] But if you want to be theologically correct, we worship the Father, through Jesus the Son, in the Holy Spirit.

Polycarp (AD 70–155) was mentored by the apostle John and later became Bishop of Smyrna. He expressed his worship of God the Trinity like this, in a beautiful, ancient prayer of the church:

O Lord God Almighty . . . I bless you and glorify you through the eternal and heavenly High Priest, Jesus Christ, your beloved Son, through whom be glory to you, with him and the Holy Spirit, both now and for ever.

ACTION: Read the story of Jesus' baptism, beginning at Matthew 3:13. Take some time, reading it slowly and a few times. Write down what you notice about the three persons of God and how they work together in this amazing story. Then remind yourself that God the Trinity is still at work today – in the world and in your life.

PRAYER: Pray the prayer of Polycarp at the end of today's chapter. Allow yourself to be thankful that we have a Trinitarian God of such love. Pray that you will be filled afresh with his love today. That you will live it. And give it. That in your work and relationships today you will seek to love as God loves – deeply, gladly and constantly. Pray for the resources of heaven today – the resources that come from God the Trinity. He longs to give to you.

U is for Underprivileged

We live in an unequal world. Many live in poverty. The Bible says that out of compassion, followers of Jesus should especially care for the poor and underprivileged. That's why **U is for Underprivileged**.

Every Thursday afternoon for a number of years now, the doors of The Belfrey Hall in York are opened and many homeless and lonely people are welcomed in. People chat over a hot drink and after a short message of God's love a nourishing free meal is served. Community is formed, relationships are built and lives are touched. This is one of many simple and good ways that the underprivileged in York are helped and supported.

Looking after the poor has always been important to God[1] and something he's called his followers to do. From the earliest days God's people have heard his call that justice must not be denied to those in need[2] and that an open hand of friendship should be extended to the underprivileged.[3] The people of Israel even sang of these things in their worship, declaring: 'Blessed are those who care for the weak; the LORD delivers them in times of trouble.'[4] Jesus modelled this for his followers in both the way he lived and the things he said.[5] While he loved all people, he had a bias to the poor and those who struggled in life.[6] This emphasis continued into the church, with the famous Jerusalem Council affirming that one of the few things that Gentile (i.e. non-Jewish) disciples must do was 'continue to remember the poor'.[7]

The novelist John Grisham is a follower of Christ and gives much of his money to church and to social action projects (see **M is for Mission**). When asked about this he said: 'Jesus preached more and taught more about helping the poor and the sick and the hungry than he did about heaven and hell. Shouldn't that tell us something?'[8]

Looking back in church history, the church has sometimes forgotten or neglected God's call to care for the underprivileged. Interestingly, when there's a fresh move of the Holy Spirit, this emphasis is normally renewed.[9] The social reformer William Wilberforce, for instance, who grew up near York and worked tirelessly to see the slave trade abolished in the British Empire, was a disciple of Christ who came to faith in the evangelical revival of the eighteenth century. In that same evangelical revival, William Richardson, who was a faithful predecessor of mine as vicar of The Belfrey (pastoring our church from 1771 to 1821), set up the Sunday school movement in York, which cared for and gave basic education to many poor children in the city. Richardson also spent much time visiting prisoners in jail and those who had stumbled in life because of a difficult upbringing. Caring for the underprivileged in this way is central to the ministry of the Spirit and is catalysed in revival. As Bill Johnson says, 'Defending the defenceless and speaking for those who have no voice are a huge part of the effects of revival.'[10]

Caring for the poor is a key sign of God's kingdom[11] (see **K is for Kingdom**). It's an essential part of God's clear call that disciples should 'do good',[12] showing the Father's love. Along with other signs and wonders, it's part of what a giving (see **G is for Giving**), Spirit-filled community of disciples should be doing.[13] As God pours out his Spirit afresh, we should expect to see all sorts of new ways of caring for the underprivileged emerge (see **N is for New**). At The Belfrey we've recently begun to provide clothes and toys for underprivileged parents who need these things for their babies and toddlers. There was no work like it in the city and Rachel, a caring mum in our church, saw the need, felt a call and stepped in. It's another sign of the kingdom of God.

All such care must be motivated by genuine love and compassion.[14] Disciples mustn't do this from any other motive and it mustn't be done in a patronizing or judgemental manner. It doesn't win God's love (as he can't love us any more or less) but it does please him.[15] Followers of Jesus care for the poor simply out of kindness and with a desire to care with a holistic love for all those in need. It's loving like Jesus.

Caring for the underprivileged is part and parcel of discipleship and central to the mission of the church (see **M is for Mission** and **C is for Church**). It's an important and practical aspect of demonstrating the kingdom of God in action.[16] Every disciple is called to this.

U is for Underprivileged

ACTION: Look back at your life over the last few months. What have you done to care for the underprivileged? Make a list. If your list has very few things, resolve to do something in the next few days to show God's love in this way. Find out what your local church (or group of churches) is doing to care for the poor and make a decision to do something to help.

PRAYER: Pray for at least one person you know who has given their life to especially serve the poor and vulnerable and marginalized. Give thanks for them. Pray that the Lord will continue to sustain and resource them. Pray for guidance about how you might encourage them and then make sure you do it.

V is for Vision

'If you don't know where you're going, any road will get you there,' said the Cheshire Cat in *Alice in Wonderland*. But disciples of Jesus are *not* direction-less. Rather they're called and commissioned by Christ to go and make a massive difference in the world. To help disciples in this task, the Spirit of Jesus normally gives a vision to follow. That's why **V is for Vision**.

Church leader Bill Hybels describes vision as 'a picture of the future that produces passion'.[1] That's helpful. It shows us that faith is needed for vision to come alive (see **F is for Faith**). When God gives vision, we see the future. We're at 'A', but we see the 'B' we need to get to, and it thrills us. That's having vision.

The Bible is full of examples of God giving people vision. From Abraham – the father of faith[2] – who was told to leave his home and journey to a promised land,[3] to the apostle Paul, who was called to bring the good news of Jesus to Gentiles,[4] God gives vision to those he calls.

Jesus had the biggest vision of all – it was 'the kingdom of God'[5] (see **K is for Kingdom**) breaking into lives in the here and now and impacting planet earth.[6] As disciples our vision(s) must be part of this wider vision, as we pray, with Christ, that the 'kingdom [would] come, on earth as it is in heaven'.[7]

Our good God gives personal vision to each of us, for our lives, loved ones, workplaces and much more, helping us see the way ahead.[8] He also gives vision to families. To churches.

To communities. Even to cities, regions and nations.[9] Disciples of Jesus need to be attentive to the guidance of the Spirit[10] so we see and hear the biblically inspired vision he's giving us.

For a number of years I've kept a quote next to my desk which says: 'Make your small decisions in the light of the big picture.'[11] It reminds me to keep the vision central. The vision – the big picture – gives direction. Strategy helps us get there. God would need to communicate clearly and confirm it a number of times in order for me to change the 'big picture' vision, but I don't need to keep waiting to hear from God when making the smaller decisions. I can simply offer them to God, praying for his help to live wisely and that he'll give me discernment (see **H is for Holy Spirit**) as I live within the parameters of the vision he's already given.

Our vision as a family since Sam and I married has always been short and simple: 'As for me and my household, we will serve the LORD.'[12] But a household might prayerfully agree a fuller vision which, for example, might be 'to know God better together, to help each other to thrive, and to encourage respect, generosity and love'. That vision will shape the decisions they make, how they treat each other, the kind of conversations they have, and much more.

At The Belfrey in York, our vision is to play our part in 'serving God's transformation of the North'. That means we feel a love and responsibility not just for the 200,000 people of our city but for the 15 million people in our region and we want to do all we can to see the north of England revived – with more and more people becoming disciples and the kingdom of God impacting all aspects of life.

However, keeping the vision clear and making sure we don't get distracted is difficult, especially when things get busy. As

Craig Groeschel says: 'busyness blurs vision.'[13] That's why we need to be sure our vision is clear and memorable[14] and we need to keep coming back and be reminded of it again and again. If you're leading anything (from a family to a nation), you'll need to keep telling people the God-given vision and keep recasting it, because vision leaks. Vision requires leadership and constant articulation. Most disciples and leaders of disciples don't do this enough. Don't forget that constant bombardment produces impact!

When considering a church to join, it's good to hear their vision. Where are they going? Are you happy to go on this journey with them? If not, find another community to join.

What happens when there is no vision? Or when it's unclear or confused? Proverbs 29:18 says that 'where there is no vision, the people perish' (KJV). Lack of vision is the death of us! We might as well not exist. This is a stark reminder that disciples are not here just to take up space. We're people on a mission (see **M is for Mission**). We're called to follow Christ and to go and change the world with the vision God gives us.[15]

What a privilege. And what a responsibility.

V is for Vision

ACTION: Consider if there's an area of your life where the vision and direction is blurred and unclear. If so, write it down with the intention of doing something about it. Has God been saying anything relevant about this recently (e.g. as you've been reading the Bible, or through a prophetic word)? If so, write it down.

PRAYER: Then pray and ask the Lord to bring clarity of vision in this area. You might find clarity comes as you pray, or you may need more time to consider this over the next few days and weeks. If it's a matter that involves others, do talk with them about it, as corporate vision needs to be shared and embraced. Cover all this in prayer, trusting that the Lord will guide you. When it's clear, make sure it's written down. Then go, and do it – empowered by the Holy Spirit.

W is for Worship

We worship what we love. That means that everyone worships something, whether they realize it or not. Disciples worship Jesus. So worship is essential to who we are and what we do. That's why **W is for Worship**.

The Bible encourages us not to give half-hearted devotion to God but rather to give him our best.[1] After all, he gave us the best thing he had when he sent his Son, Jesus Christ, into the world (see **J is for Jesus**) and we should do the same. The best thing we have is ourselves. As we give our lives to Christ to be used daily in his service, the Bible calls this 'true and proper worship'.[2] Christ, who became the Great Sacrifice,[3] calls disciples to lay down their lives and serve him as a living sacrifice.

Worship, however, is not limited to living lives devoted to Christ. It also describes the very act of adoration.[4] It includes times of worship, as disciples spend time drawing close to God, giving him praise and love. A great example of this is seen in the story of the Wise Men who travelled thousands of miles from the East to worship the infant Jesus. After a difficult but rewarding journey they eventually find him, and as they see him we're told that 'they bowed down and worshipped him'.[5] The Greek word used there for worship literally means 'to come towards to kiss'. It describes intimacy and love. When disciples spend time worshipping Jesus, that's exactly what they're doing – expressing adoration.

As we worship the Lord in intimacy, so we often encounter the presence of the Holy Spirit.[6] We draw near to him and he draws near to us[7] and we experience his love. However, we don't worship God in order to experience him – although that is often what happens as a consequence. Instead we worship him because he deserves our praise. He is worthy of it all.[8] At all times in all places. These times of worship sustain a life of worship.

God loves our worship. He doesn't need it. Without it he is no less God. But it does give him pleasure and he knows it's good for us, because through it we are changed. Tom Wright expresses this well when he says: 'You become like what you worship. When you gaze in awe, admiration, and wonder at something or someone, you begin to take on something of the character of the object of your worship.'[9] Worship leads to transformation.

We can worship God on our own. In our families. In small groups. In congregations. All are important and helpful in different ways. The Bible has much to say about worshipping together,[10] and disciples are particularly told not to give up meeting with others.[11] History teaches that when a disciple does this then invariably his or her faith begins to go cold, like an ember being taken away from coals on a fire. But place the coal back on the fire and it soon begins to glow again!

Disciples should never be embarrassed about spending time in worship with God. As we sing our songs to him and tell him how much we appreciate him, our vision of him expands and our love for him grows.[12] Of course his love for us is much greater and stronger than ours for him, but nevertheless all disciples are called to give God our love.[13] I've noticed that worshippers in some churches seem to get rather disinterested after a few minutes of doing this. If they're married, I hope they don't get similarly bored after just a few minutes of telling their spouse how much they love them! Also, they're in for a shock when they get to heaven! We're going to spend a long time there in worship, and we'll never get tired. That's why it's important to give time and space to adoring our loving Father, this side of heaven. He doesn't need it, but he loves it. And it's good for us.[14] When we worship, we're allowing God's word to sink into our hearts.[15] We're building each other up.[16] We're making war.[17] We're strengthening ourselves.[18] We're having our perspectives realigned.[19] We're being filled with joy.[20] We're glorifying God.[21]

Giving is key to worship (see **G is for Giving**). It's an active choice. A definite decision. Even if circumstances are difficult or we don't feel like it.[22] God deserves our worship, so we intentionally give it. Sometimes this might feel like 'a sacrifice of praise'.[23]

Often our worship begins with praise. Because God is a good Father[24] we can praise him with vigour, enthusiasm, determination and zeal (see **Z is for Zeal**). Over the years, I've been asked on a number of occasions to spend time with schoolchildren from local schools wanting to visit a church to learn more about what happens there. I'm often fascinated to see the teachers telling the children to be quiet or to whisper in church. The children probably wonder who they're hiding from! The Bible has something rather different to say about coming into God's house. We're told when we come to worship that we should rejoice,[25] clap,[26] dance,[27] shout,[28] extol (which means praise enthusiastically),[29] kneel[30] and adore[31] our good Father (and much more!). Outside church, we're to be people who 'rejoice always, pray continually, give thanks in all circumstances'.[32] So at all times and in all places we're called to live a life of passionate worship!

William Temple, one of the great Anglican archbishops of the last century, said that worship is 'to quicken the conscience by the holiness of God, to feed the mind with the truth of God, to purge the imagination by the beauty of God, to open up the heart to the love of God, to devote the will to the purpose of God'.[33] That's why to truly worship God is a tremendous honour and privilege. It is, as David Watson has said, 'the primary task of the Christian'.[34]

ACTION: Read the story of the Wise Men (Matthew 2:1–12) and write down your reflections on their worship. Then read Romans 12:1–2 and write your thoughts on living a life of worship.

PRAYER: Re-read what you have written today and turn it into prayer. Give thanks to Jesus for his love and give your adoration to him. Then tell him that he can have your life – every part of it. Finally pray for your church, that its worship would be Christ-centred, celebratory, intimate and loving.

$\boxed{\text{X}}$ is for X-rated

There are some things in life that are no-go areas for disciples of Jesus.

In the same way that I, as a loving parent, discourage my children from certain things because I don't want to see them get hurt, so God tells us to avoid certain things for our benefit. Wise disciples soon discover that not everything that's available to us on planet earth is good or healthy.[1] In fact from the earliest days of the faith, the church has taught that not everything is beneficial and that there are certain things 'you will do well to avoid'.[2] They're no-go areas.[3] X-rated.[4] That's why **X is for X-rated**.

When we consider X-rated things, many people think first about sex (as sexually explicit films used to be rated 'X' in a UK cinema). However, sex in itself isn't an X-rated subject for God – in fact, quite the opposite.

God loves sex. After all, he invented it! He inspired a whole book of the Bible about it (called the Song of Songs) and thoroughly approves of fun-filled sexual love shared between a wife and husband. He gives a lot of freedom for a couple to enjoy pleasure and tenderness within a loving heterosexual marriage. But anything outside those boundaries is, according to the Bible, sexual sin – what some Bibles translate as 'fornication' – and it's a no-go, X-rated area for disciples. That includes sex before marriage,[5] extramarital affairs[6] and same-sex activity.[7] It would also include other practices such as sexual activity with more than your spouse[8] and bestiality.[9] Although the Bible is not explicit on it, most church leaders advise married couples to avoid both sado-masochistic and anal sex.

Viewing pornographic material is also X-rated. It encourages lust rather than love.[10] Most women involved in the so-called 'adult entertainment industry' are exploited. Research shows that viewers of porn often end up with an unhelpful and unrealistic view of sex and a distorted perception of members of the opposite sex.

Twenty-first-century western culture has very few sexual boundaries, but disciples are called to live differently – within the boundaries given by the Creator. Our loving Father made sex to be good, but some kinds of sex are not good.[11] Disciples need to understand the difference.

Some people who've been involved in some of these X-rated sexual practices feel particularly guilty and dirty about it. God doesn't see people in that way, and neither should disciples. There's no place for judgementalism. All can come to Christ for forgiveness and a new start.[12]

Disciples are called to be peace-loving and peace-making people.[13] Encouraging violence and watching it on TV or in movies is not good and should best be avoided.[14] Horror movies and sadistic films and literature are similarly X-rated.[15]

Any form of exploitation of another person is also a huge no-go area for disciples, and this includes sexual, psychological, emotional and financial exploitation.[16] Rather, disciples are called to set free those who are caught up in injustices in the world, like human trafficking and abuse.[17] Exploitation normally involves misuse of power,[18] and followers of Christ, seeking to live humbly, need to take particular care when working with children,[19] women,[20] vulnerable adults, and any others where power dynamics can be mistaken, manipulated or misused.

Disciples, like all people, can find themselves exploiting the environment. The Bible says that God placed human beings on earth to steward and manage the earth's resources.[21] Misuse of the planet should be avoided if at all possible and sustainable living encouraged[22] in the light of the best scientific advice available.

Getting drunk on alcohol, or using drugs or non-prescription highs, is also X-rated for believers.[23] These activities often lead to addiction and are not good for our souls. They negatively impact others and are a substitute for being full of the Holy Spirit.[24]

If Christ-followers are going to take discipleship seriously then care is needed over words spoken.[25] The Bible says we should only speak words which build others up (see **E is for Encourage**). That means we need to be careful about what we say, how we say it and where we say it.[26] There's no place for gossip,[27] for tearing others down or for using disrespectful language.[28] If in doubt, stay quiet![29] Certainly we should avoid bad language and if this is a problem then get some prayer to help you stop swearing! Words are powerful and important, and they reveal our hearts.[30]

As a church leader I spend some of my time helping and pastoring people through these X-rated issues. I don't think any less of people who struggle with these things. Indeed for many disciples these are ongoing issues that are sometimes difficult to master, so having accountable relationships (see **C is for Church**) and asking for the help of the Holy Spirit (see **H is for Holy Spirit**) are vital if progress is to be made. As more and more people join the church these days from a background of no faith, we're going to increasingly find people starting the journey of discipleship bringing quite a lot of baggage with them. That's why we need to be clear, frank, polite, supportive and caring as we talk about and pray through these issues.

It's important for disciples to remember this: whatever we take into our lives is what eventually comes out.[31] If we take in rubbish, then rubbish will fill us and will spill out of us. That's why the Bible gives this simple but helpful advice: 'Whatever is true, whatever is noble, whatever is right, whatever is pure, whatever is lovely, whatever is admirable – if anything is excellent or praiseworthy – think about such things.'[32]

ACTION: Look back over this chapter again. Is there an area which is not right in your life? Something you need to change? Something X-rated you need to stop? Or something more positive you should be starting? Allow the Spirit of God to search your heart. He will not condemn you, but he may convict you. Be honest. If necessary, confess and repent, and vow to change. Write down what you resolve to do.

PRAYER: Thank the Lord that he loves us and, like a good Father, wants good things for us. Thank him for sending Jesus to forgive us and give a brand-new start. If there are things to put right with God, make sure you do that. If it involves others who you need to go and see, ask the Holy Spirit to make you brave to do this and to do it well. It sometimes helps to talk in confidence with another disciple about some of these matters. Ask God if there is someone you can approach to be accountable to, someone who will encourage you as you seek to make progress. Finally, pray for someone known to you who is caught up in some X-rated area. Pray for love for them and that you might be a means of helping them live life better – as God intends.

$\boxed{\text{Y}}$ is for Yes!

The Bible is a book full of promises. The promises become ours as we hear them, believe them, pray them and live them. These promises, disciples are told, are all 'Yes' and 'Amen' in Christ.[1] That's why **Y is for Yes!**

Some people think that God is cross. They perceive him looking at humanity through a negative lens. They see him as a tyrannical rule-maker who's angry at our disobedience. They think God really doesn't like us very much and certainly doesn't want us to enjoy life. But nothing could be further from the truth. God loves us and loves life! Jesus said he came that we might 'have life, and have it to the full'.[2] This filled, overflowing life of the disciple is meant to be daring and courageous and fun and attractive!

As we saw in **X is for X-rated**, there are some things in life that are worth avoiding – things God says 'no' to. This isn't because God is a killjoy. In fact he says 'no' to these bad things because he says 'yes' to their greater opposites – which are all good things. Let me explain. God says 'no' to pornography because he says 'yes' to great, loving sex in marriage.[3] He says 'no' to lying because he says 'yes' to speaking the truth.[4] He says 'no' to getting drunk because he says 'yes' to being filled with the Holy Spirit.[5]

As a father to my sons, I want them all to thrive. I want to give them all I can to help them to live life well. If they come and ask me for something, unless I know it's bad for them,

I want the answer to be 'yes', if possible. Why? Because I love them! But I'm very aware that I do all that imperfectly, and that the best model for fathering is found in God the Father[6] (see **A is for Abba**), the One who is 'for us', not 'against us'.[7] He wants to bless us, not curse us.[8] He wants to encourage us, not discourage us.[9] He wants to heal us, not hurt us.[10] We can trust him.

God's word, the Bible, includes many promises that apply to our lives today[11] (see **B is for Bible**). They are all good.[12] And our good Father is faithful and trustworthy to every one.[13] They are a record of him saying 'yes' over and over again to us. Because he loves us. And because he wants us to live life well and to thrive,[14] and to help others do the same.[15]

If God is like this, it should cause us to live for him,[16] pray to him (see **P is for Prayer**) and be like him.[17] As we meditate on his promises,[18] disciples are called to be trustworthy, positive, helpful and encouraging (see **E is for Encourage**). We're supposed to be the most positive people anyone will meet, empowering others to live as God intends.

When David, my youngest son, was still at primary school, I invited the head teacher of his school to come to speak to our church's staff team. I did this because that school was the most positive community I had ever come across. Over a number of years the head had encouraged the children to see that they were gifted, that they could excel, that they could achieve and grow and develop and do amazing things. As a result the pupils were performing well and the school was flourishing. I wanted us to learn from the positive culture he'd built at that school, and so invited him in to share his approach with us, in order that the culture we were creating among The Belfrey staff might be even more 'Yes' and 'Amen!'

I'm privileged to work with a gifted and enthusiastic staff team at The Belfrey. In order to maintain and encourage positivity, when we employ new staff we often write into the Person Specification that we're looking for someone with 'a can-do attitude'. That's because we're not looking for pessimistic, unwilling, negative people. Not moaners and groaners. Because in Jesus Christ we're set free from such a mindset. Disciples might even find themselves in prison, but like Paul and Silas in Acts 16, they can confidently sing songs of praise,[19] because God can be trusted. He is with us, and his joy is greater than any negative or difficult circumstances.

If we want to reach our God-given potential as disciples, we need much encouragement. We need to hear the stories of what God is doing among us, which build our faith (see **F is for Faith**) and give us hope. We need to read, learn and inwardly digest the trustworthy promises of God found in Scripture. As we immerse ourselves in such environments we will be transformed. And as a result we will transform those with whom we meet.

Being people of transformation is our calling. It's our destiny. All because our good God says 'yes!' to us.

Y is for Yes!

ACTION: Write down some of the promises of God you have been discovering recently. It may help to look back over what you've written previously and see if there are any promises which you've written down and now stand out for you.

PRAYER: Praise God that he is a God who keeps his promises. Begin to thank him for what he's been showing you recently. If there's a particular promise that stands out, turn it into a prayer, asking God to fulfil it in your life in the coming days. End up in worship – adoring Christ for his presence, love and provision. Pray that you will honour him with your day today, shining his light, and – like him – be a positive, encouraging 'yes' person!

$\boxed{\text{Z}}$ is for Zeal

So we get to the final chapter of the *A–Z of Discipleship* – to Z. And **Z is for Zeal**.

Zeal is about being passionate in following Jesus. Loving him with *all* your heart. It's about enthusiastically following him for the rest of life. That's my encouragement to all readers of this book. It's one thing to start well, but our Heavenly Father wants us to finish well too, filling us with his life-giving Spirit on a continual basis[1] to sustain us and help us run the race of faith to our dying day, and receive the crown of glory in heaven.[2]

Luther Porter was a disciple who finished well. He was my grandfather on my father's side of the family. When I was a boy I loved to hear Grandpa pray for he was a man steeped in years of friendship with God. Sometimes when he prayed he got rather emotional and would choke up and even weep. In my early teens I remember being a little embarrassed about this, but as I got older I saw it differently. I began to see that rather than being awkward it was actually a beautiful thing. Grandpa was simply expressing from his heart his passionate love for the God who made him, saved him and was still present with him after all these years.

If we're going to keep following Jesus for the rest of our lives, we, like my Grandpa Luther, need to stay passionate and zealous disciples! The Bible is clear that this is what disciples are called to do, saying: 'Never be lacking in zeal, but keep your spiritual fervour'.[3] There are all sorts of things we can do to help ourselves in this.

One is to keep going.[4] Even when things are tough and hard and difficult.[5] This isn't always straightforward, but it's definitely worth it.[6] In the same way that husbands and wives have to, at times, persevere when their marriages go through a difficult patch, it's the same with our relationship with Christ. It's definitely worth pressing on.[7] You won't regret it. Believe me. (And I write as one who's been following Christ now for well over thirty years.)

It's also important that we keep living our faith in word and action. A great example of this in the Bible is seen in a disciple called Phoebe. We read about her in Romans 16:1–2. Not only was she a kind and generous church worker, but she was also entrusted to carry Paul's letter to the Roman church. She showed her zeal in the way she lived and as a result was trusted and commended. The cause of the good news of Jesus is the greatest thing a person can live for, with the greatest reward. So don't stop!

Another is to do the basics well. Things like: reading the Bible (see **B is for Bible**), praying (see **P is for Prayer**), worshipping with others (see **W is for Worship**) and attending church[8] (see **C is for Church**). When we're struggling we don't feel like doing these things, and it's tempting to stop. But these are the things that will actually sustain us. So persevere! Keep going.[9]

It's also good to keep giving your best in every area of life.[10] This is where zeal becomes particularly important.[11] Being zealous is about staying committed, staying focused and positive. A great example in the Bible is a disciple called Titus, who's mentioned a number of times in the New Testament

and in 2 Corinthians is described as someone 'who has often proved . . . in many ways that he is zealous'.[12] As Christ-
followers today keep giving their best like Titus, so they find
that God gives back to them (see **G is for Giving**). That's how
it often works in the kingdom of God and is why the Bible says:
'Whoever sows sparingly will also reap sparingly, and whoever
sows generously will also reap generously.'[13]

God loves to respond to zeal and passion,[14] partly because
zeal is one of his characteristics. On a number of occasions the
Bible says that 'the zeal of the LORD Almighty will accomplish
this'.[15]

Our Father is fully committed to us (see **A is for Abba**).
Fully devoted to us. Fully supportive of us. He passionately
loves us.[16] That's why he sent Jesus to live and die for us.[17] Our
response should be to love him back, with zeal and passion.
This takes us back to the Introduction, where we began with
Jesus. Jesus Christ tells us that the *most* important thing we
can do in life is to love God with *everything* we've got: 'with
all [our] heart . . . soul . . . mind and . . . strength'.[18] This is
the zealous, passionate life that disciples are called to. Because
that's how God is with us.

I am English – a nation normally known for our lack of
emotional expression. Many English people, especially men,
find it hard to laugh or cry. But God isn't English and I'm
slowly learning to be more relaxed in expressing my emotions –
in my worship to him and in my interactions with others. After
all, if being a disciple is important then I shouldn't be afraid to
express it with passion and enthusiasm!

Our passions and emotions have been created by our good
Father and so they're good – in fact, 'very good'.[19] While we

mustn't be controlled or led by our emotions, we certainly need to recognize them and appropriately express them. What we mustn't do is fear them[20] or people's response to them.[21] Neither should we deny them, for, as Brené Brown says: 'denial of emotion is what feeds the dark.'[22] Instead we should embrace our emotions and ask the Holy Spirit to use them so others can see that the life of a disciple is a great and exciting adventure.

This doesn't mean being a disciple is easy. Often it's hard, challenging and exhausting. But there's no need to worry.[23] No need to be afraid.[24] Because 'God did not give us a Spirit of fear but of power and love and self-control'.[25] So follow Jesus with all you have and you'll never regret it. And encourage as many as you can to do the same with passion and love.

This is the life of the disciple. It's the best life. It's the life to which you are called. That's why the last chapter of the Bible says: 'The Spirit and the bride say, "Come!"'[26] So come to Christ today, and follow him.

I hope this short book has ignited a passion in you to be a disciple of Jesus Christ. My prayer for you is that you might never be lacking in zeal and that God by his Spirit will give you energy and enthusiasm to spend yourself in the pursuit of a most glorious cause – that of the good news of Jesus Christ.

ACTION: As you come to the end of this book, take stock. Do you hear Christ's call to follow him with everything you have? If so, how do you respond? I encourage you to commit or re-commit your life to him. Go back to the end of the first chapter of this *A–Z* and remind yourself of the prayer you made. Since praying that prayer, do you know the love of your good Father more fully? Are you following Christ more closely? Are you experiencing the Spirit more intimately? If you want to be a disciple for the rest of your life and then into eternity, write down the commitment you make.

PRAYER: Now turn this commitment into prayer. Tell the Lord how grateful you are for his love, his presence and his call upon your life to follow him and to make a massive difference in the world. Pray that he will fill you again with the Holy Spirit and that he'll sustain you day by day. Pray for loved ones and friends, that your zeal for Jesus Christ will spill out to them. Now ask the Spirit to bring to mind someone you can either give this book to, or send a copy to, to encourage them. Resolve to do that today. Then follow Christ for the rest of your life.

Notes

Introduction

1   David Watson, *Discipleship* (London: Hodder & Stoughton, 1981, 1987), p. 20. David Watson was a previous vicar of The Belfrey in York, the church I now lead. He was a great evangelist and Bible teacher, helping many to find faith in Christ and be filled with the Holy Spirit. He wrote a number of excellent books. His book *Discipleship* (entitled *Called and Committed* in the USA) still speaks powerfully, with a prophetic voice, calling the contemporary church and society to a radical, uncompromising following of Jesus. This book stands in that tradition, desiring the message of discipleship to be embraced by a new generation – especially those who are not yet, or are just beginning to become, followers of Jesus.

2   Rick Warren, *The Purpose Driven Life* (Grand Rapids: Zondervan, 2002), p. 17.

3   'Jesus Christ' is the founder of the Christian faith. 'Jesus' is his name, given at his birth. 'Christ' is not his surname but a description, often attached to his name, which derives from the Greek word *christos*, meaning 'Chosen One' or 'Anointed One'.

4   Christians have always believed that the life and teachings of Jesus, coupled with his sacrificial death, his resurrection from the dead and his ascension into heaven, form the foundation

of faith for the disciple. See, for example, Romans 8:34; Colossians 1:1–23.

5 John 1:1.
6 See John 1:14.
7 They called the period before his birth 'BC' – Before Christ, and the period after his birth 'AD' – *Anno Domini*, which literally means 'the year of the Lord'.
8 Colossians 1:15.
9 See John 14:9.
10 See John 14:6; Hebrews 10:20.
11 BBC Radio 4 interview in 2005, on receiving racist email after becoming the first black British archbishop.
12 See Matthew 11:28; Revelation 3:19,20; Ephesians 2:10.
13 See Matthew 16:24; 1 Peter 2:21.

A is for Abba

1 *Abba* is an Aramaic word used by Jesus and the people of his day. Aramaic is a Semitic language still used by 200,000 people today. The New Testament section of the Bible was written in Greek but includes some Aramaic, including this word *Abba*. While used by infants, *Abba* is not a childish word. An adult would use it as an intimate word for his or her father.
2 See Deuteronomy 32:6; Isaiah 64:8; Malachi 2:10; John 14:9–11; 1 Corinthians 8:6.
3 See 1 Peter 1:3.
4 Mark 14:36.
5 Matthew 6:9.
6 See Matthew 7:11.
7 John 4:24.
8 See Ephesians 1:3.
9 See Genesis 1:25.
10 See Psalm 8.

[11] Genesis 1:31.

[12] Genesis 1:27.

[13] See Genesis 1:28–30.

[14] See Genesis 3; Romans 3:23; 1 John 1:9.

[15] See 1 John 5:17.

[16] See Psalm 42:3; Acts 17:27.

[17] See Romans 4:25.

[18] See 1 John 3:1.

[19] See Romans 8:15; John 1:12–13.

[20] See Ephesians 2:18.

[21] See 2 Corinthians 5:20.

[22] See Ephesians 1:18.

[23] Romans 8:17.

[24] See John 14:9.

[25] See Hebrews 12:4–11.

[26] See Matthew 7:7–12.

[27] See John 16:13.

[28] See www.alpha.org. There are helpful online films and resources and a number of excellent books written by Nicky Gumbel, associated with Alpha; see especially Nicky Gumbel, *Questions of Life* (London: Alpha, 1993, 2010).

B is for Bible

[1] 'Apocalyptic' is a special form of prophetic literature that usually focuses on the 'end times' and often includes visions and revelations.

[2] See Hebrews 4:12; Ephesians 6:17; Matthew 4:4; Isaiah 55:11; Psalm 12:6.

[3] Psalm 119:105.

[4] See John 16:13.

[5] See 2 Timothy 3:16–17.

[6] That's why some Bibles say 'Holy Bible' on the cover.

Notes

7 In many churches, after the Bible has been read, the reader says: 'This is the word of the Lord.'

8 See 2 Peter 3:16.

9 Leaders of the European Reformation in the sixteenth century, who called the church to return to the Bible as the main source of authority, described this as 'the perspicuity of Scripture'.

10 See Matthew 5:17.

11 For example: the kingdom of God is no longer extended by taking physical land through war and bloodshed, but through love, with lives being won for Christ as new disciples are made (see Matthew 5:44; 28:19). The enemy, for the disciple of Jesus, is not another human being but the devil and evil (see Ephesians 6:12). Blood sacrifices cease because Christ fulfilled everything they were pointing to and became the final sacrifice (see Hebrews 9:12). The priesthood that stood between worshipper and God has ceased (see Hebrews 7:23–24). The physical temple is no longer the geographic centre of worship (see Matthew 18:20). The food and purity laws that set Israel apart have been fulfilled (see Mark 7:18–19).

12 Leonard Ravenhill, *Why Revival Tarries* (Bloomington, MN: Bethany House, 1959, 1987), p. 71.

13 For example, the context and resulting application of Mark 9:40 is very different from that of Matthew 12:30.

14 On women in leadership, for example, see 1 Timothy 2:12 where women are told to 'be quiet', whereas 1 Corinthians 11:5 says women can prophesy. Romans 16:7 goes further, telling of Junia, who seems to be a female apostle and senior leader.

15 See Hebrews 4:12.

16 See Revelation 22:18–19. While in its original context this is referring to the book of Revelation, many take these words, which now come at the very end of the Bible, to refer to the Bible as a whole.

17 See Matthew 6:10.

18 Bill Johnson, *When Heaven Invades Earth* (Shippensburg, PA: Destiny Image, 2003), p. 163.

C is for Church

[1] See Genesis 2:18.
[2] See Mark 12:30–31.
[3] See Ephesians 2:21.
[4] See 1 Corinthians 3:9.
[5] Nicky Gumbel, Twitter, 15 May 2016.
[6] Colossians 1:15–16.
[7] Colossians 1:18 (my emphasis).
[8] See Revelation 21:9; 2 Corinthians 11:2; Ephesians 5:25–27.
[9] See Acts 2:42.
[10] David Watson, to Church Redundancy Committee, on the future of St Cuthbert's York (1965).
[11] See Ephesians 3:10.
[12] See Acts 1:8.
[13] See Matthew 28:18–20.

D is for Disciplines

[1] See Richard Foster, *Celebration of Discipline* (London: Hodder & Stoughton, 2008).
[2] Wesley required Methodist church leadership candidates to fast at least two days per week.
[3] It's possible to fast from all sorts of different things. The Bible especially mentions fasting from alcohol (see Leviticus 10:9; Luke 1:15) and married people fasting for a time from sex (see 1 Corinthians 7:5).
[4] Normally on Wednesdays and Fridays, although it was not obligatory. Others chose to fast for one day per month or on particular holy days.
[5] See Ezra 8:21.
[6] See Joel 2:12.
[7] See Judges 20:26.

Notes

8 See Ezra 8:22.
9 See 2 Chronicles 20:3.
10 See Psalm 35:13.
11 See Acts 13:2–3.
12 See Mark 9:29.
13 See Jonah 3:6–10.
14 See Daniel 10:2–6.
15 See Matthew 4:2.
16 'When you fast . . .' (Matthew 6:16).
17 See Isaiah 58:1–10.
18 Source unknown.

E is for Encourage

1 See Romans 14:19.
2 See Colossians 2:2.
3 See Romans 12:10.
4 See Hebrews 13:7.
5 1 Thessalonians 5:11.
6 See Philippians 2:3.
7 See Acts 16:40.
8 See 1 Samuel 30:6.
9 See Colossians 3:16.
10 Ephesians 4:15.
11 See Luke 10:38; John 11:1–45.
12 1 Thessalonians 5:18.
13 See Habakkuk 3:17–18; Philippians 4:12–13.
14 See Nehemiah 8:10.
15 See Psalm 68:35.
16 See Philippians 1:18–19.
17 See 1 Peter 1:6.
18 See Ephesians 5:20.
19 See John 8:44.

[20] Acts 4:36.
[21] Acts 11:23.
[22] Acts 11:24a.
[23] See Acts 11:24b.

F is for Faith

[1] See Hebrews 11:1.
[2] See Luke 5:20.
[3] See Matthew 17:20.
[4] See Luke 17:5–10.
[5] See Romans 10:17.
[6] See John 3:3.
[7] See Matthew 13:33.
[8] See Romans 4:16.
[9] See Genesis 12 – 25.
[10] See Habakkuk 3:2.
[11] See 2 Thessalonians 1:3; Colossians 1:9–10; Ephesians 4:12–13.
[12] See Matthew 17:20.

G is for Giving

[1] See Ephesians 2:8–9.
[2] See James 4:6.
[3] See 1 Timothy 2:4.
[4] See Matthew 10:8.
[5] See James 1:5; John 3:34.
[6] 2 Corinthians 8:7 describes the 'grace of giving'.
[7] See 2 Corinthians 9:11.
[8] It even predates the giving of the Law (see Genesis 14:18–20). While Jesus criticizes religious leaders for tithing without showing

justice, mercy and faithfulness, he nevertheless commends the practice (Matthew 23:23).

9 See 2 Corinthians 9:7.

10 Luke 8:3.

11 See Luke 12:13–21.

12 Adam Grant, *Give and Take* (New York: Penguin, 2013).

13 See Luke 21:1–4.

14 Luke 6:38.

H is for Holy Spirit

1 This is a helpful phrase used by church leader and author Gordon Fee to describe the Holy Spirit.

2 Speaking in tongues is praying in an unlearned, God-given language. It's a gift of the Holy Spirit, used mainly for personal prayer and worship, and to build up the believer. It's a basic gift, not a gift for 'advanced' disciples. Like all God's gifts, it's still available today. Teaching on this gift is particularly found in 1 Corinthians 12 and 14.

3 When Ephesians 5:18 says 'be filled with the Spirit', the tense is present continuous, meaning 'be filled again and again'.

4 In the history of the church there's been some debate as to whether being baptized in the Spirit is a second and separate event to becoming a Christian. For many it can be, but the book of Acts shows it doesn't have to be. The most important thing is that disciples know they are following Jesus and are full of the Spirit today.

5 See 1 Peter 1:16.

6 See John 16:8. Conviction is not the same as condemnation. The Spirit of God convicts us, for our encouragement – to help us become more like Christ. The devil condemns us, for our discouragement.

7 See Galatians 5:22–23.

8   See Romans 8:9; Acts 16:7.
9   See Luke 4:1.
10 See Ephesians 1:19–20.
11 See Luke 4:18–19.
12 See 2 Corinthians 3:17.
13 See 1 Corinthians 6:19.
14 See Psalm 104:30a.
15 See Genesis 1:2.
16 See Psalm 104:30b.
17 Bezalel (see Exodus 31:1–5).
18 See Acts 2:38.
19 See Acts 2:47; 19:1–20.
20 See Luke 11:13.
21 See 1 Corinthians 14:1.
22 James 1:5.
23 See, for example, Proverbs 1:20–33; 8:1 – 9:6.
24 Ephesians 1:17a.
25 See Ephesians 1:17b.
26 See Colossians 4:5–6.
27 See Proverbs 3.
28 See Philippians 1:9–10.
29 See 2 Chronicles 1:10.
30 See 1 Kings 3:16–28.
31 See Psalm 104:24; Exodus 35:35.
32 See Proverbs 24:4.
33 See 1 Timothy 2:1–2.
34 See Romans 11:33–36.
35 See 1 Corinthians 14:3.
36 1 Corinthians 14:1.
37 See 1 Thessalonians 5:19–21.
38 See 1 Corinthians 13.
39 See John 16:14–15.
40 When God pours out the Spirit, church is formed. See Acts 2.
41 See Romans 5:5.
42 See Matthew 22:35–40.

Notes

I is for Identity

1. Nicky Gumbel, Twitter, 6 May 2016.
2. See Ephesians 1:13.
3. See Isaiah 62:3; 1 Peter 2:9a.
4. See John 3:16.
5. See 1 John 4:11.
6. See 1 Peter 2:9b.
7. See 1 John 3:8.
8. See Hebrews 2:14–15.
9. See Revelation 20.
10. John 10:10.
11. See James 4:7.
12. See 2 Corinthians 10:3.
13. See Ephesians 6:18–20.
14. See James 4:6–10.
15. See Luke 6:27; 10:25–37.
16. John 8:44.
17. See Matthew 4:1–11.
18. See Ephesians 6:11. The enemy's tactics are not just personal but at times also corporate, influencing organizations, businesses, communities and nations. The need for wise and discerning leadership in every sphere of life is crucial.
19. 'The adversary' is one biblical metaphor used for the devil (see 1 Peter 5:8). 'The Advocate' is a metaphor used by Jesus to describe the Holy Spirit (see John 14:16).
20. See Luke 4:14.
21. 1 Peter 2:9a.

J is for Jesus

1. See Romans 5:5.
2. See 1 John 4:19.
3. See Romans 8:37–39; Psalm 136:1.

[4] John Stott, *The Incomparable Christ* (Nottingham: IVP, 2014).

[5] Letter to Mme N.D. Fonvisin (1854), in *Letters of Fyodor Michailovitch Dostoevsky to His Family and Friends* (trans. Ethel Golburn Mayne; London: Chatto and Windus, 1914, 1917), Letter XXI, p. 71.

[6] See Colossians 1:15.

[7] See John 1:14.

[8] See Luke 7:36–48.

[9] See Isaiah 53; 2 Corinthians 5:21.

[10] See Mark 2:17.

[11] See Luke 19:10.

[12] See Mark 1:17.

[13] See John 3:5.

[14] See John 15:13.

[15] See Hebrews 2:14.

[16] See Acts 1:1–11.

[17] See Acts 2:33.

[18] See Matthew 6:10.

[19] See Philippians 2:9.

[20] See Acts 7:55.

[21] See Romans 8:34.

[22] See Hebrews 4:15.

[23] See John 14:9–11.

[24] See Mark 1:27.

[25] See 1 Corinthians 11:1; John 13:15.

[26] See Matthew 1:21.

[27] See Matthew 1:23.

[28] See Luke 1:35.

[29] See John 5:27.

[30] See Isaiah 9:6.

[31] See Revelation 5:5.

[32] See John 1:29.

[33] See Isaiah 9:6.

[34] See Luke 17:13.

[35] See John 8:12.

[36] See Ephesians 2:20.

37 See Acts 3:14.
38 See 1 Timothy 6:15.
39 See Ephesians 1:22.
40 See John 1:1; Revelation 19:13.
41 See John 6:35.
42 See John 10:11.
43 See John 11:25.
44 See John 15:1.
45 See John 14:6.
46 See 1 Corinthians 10:4.
47 See Hebrews 2:17.
48 See Acts 10:36.
49 See 1 John 5:20.
50 See Revelation 1:8.
51 See 2 Corinthians 4:5.
52 See 2 Corinthians 5:20.
53 See Matthew 28:18.
54 See John 14:13.
55 See Luke 10:17; Acts 3:6.
56 See Acts 1:11; 1 Thessalonians 3:13.
57 Philippians 2:10.
58 See Romans 10:9; Philippians 2:11.
59 See Acts 4:31.
60 See Acts 4:12.
61 See 1 John 4:14.

K is for Kingdom

1 Bill Johnson, *The Supernatural Power of a Transformed Mind* (Shippensburg, PA: Destiny Image, 2005), pp. 32–3.
2 Mark 1:15.
3 See Matthew 10:7.
4 See Matthew 26:29.
5 See Isaiah 61:1; Matthew 12:28.

6 Matthew 6:10.
7 See Revelation 11:15.
8 See Revelation 21:3–4.
9 See, for example, Mark 6:7–13; Matthew 10:8.
10 See Matthew 6:33.
11 See 2 Corinthians 6:1.
12 Tom Wright, *Surprised by Hope* (London: SPCK, 2011), p. 157.
13 This was occasionally the experience of Jesus too (see Mark 8:23–25).
14 See Acts 28:31.
15 See Revelation 11:15.

L is for Love

1 See 1 John 4:16.
2 See 1 John 4:7.
3 See Romans 5:5.
4 See 1 John 4:10.
5 See 1 John 4:18.
6 See Romans 14:17.
7 Tom Wright, *Mark for Everyone* (London: SPCK, 2001, 2004), p. 209.
8 See 1 Peter 4:8.
9 See Luke 6:35.
10 See Philippians 1:9.
11 See 1 Corinthians 16:14.
12 See 1 Corinthians 13:7.
13 See 1 Peter 4:8.
14 See 1 Thessalonians 5:14.
15 See John 15:12–13.
16 See 1 John 3:18.
17 See John 3:16.
18 See Mark 12:30–31.

M is for Mission

1. Matthew 28:19–20 (author's own translation).
2. See, for example, Genesis 12:1; Jeremiah 2:1–4; Jonah 1:1–2; Acts 9:11–12; 22:21.
3. Emil Brunner, *The Word and the World* (London: Student Christian Movement, 1931), p. 108.
4. See 2 Corinthians 5:14.
5. Theologians call this the *missio dei* – the 'mission of God'. See 2 Corinthians 5:20.
6. Steve Addison, *Movements that Change the World* (Smyrna, DE: Missional Press, 2009), p. 115.
7. See Matthew 10:5–8.
8. Mark 1:15.
9. See 1 Peter 3:15b.
10. Ephesians 4:11.
11. See 1 John 3:18.
12. Heidi Baker, *Compelled by Love* (Lake Mary, FL: Charisma House, 2008), p. 35.
13. See Galatians 2:7–10.
14. See Matthew 5:14–16.
15. For example: William Wilberforce, Elizabeth Fry, Florence Nightingale, Martin Luther King, Mother Teresa of Calcutta.
16. Matthew 25:21.

N is for New

1. See John 3:7.
2. Revelation 21:5.
3. See Isaiah 65:17–25.
4. See Ephesians 4:22–24.
5. See Psalm 103:2.
6. See Genesis 1:1.

7 See Psalm 19:1.
8 See Hebrews 11:10.
9 See Hebrews 12:2.
10 See Isaiah 43:18–19; Acts 5:20.
11 See Psalm 33:3; Revelation 5:9.
12 See Mark 5:19; Revelation 12:11.
13 See Psalm 105:2.
14 2 Corinthians 5:17 (NIV 1984).
15 See Romans 6:4.
16 See Galatians 5:22–23.
17 See Romans 12:2.
18 See Galatians 2:20.
19 See 2 Corinthians 4:16–18.
20 Revelation 21:2.
21 Revelation 21:1.
22 See 2 Corinthians 5:1–5.
23 See Revelation 22:3.
24 See John 14:2.
25 See Revelation 21:4.
26 See Daniel 2:21; Ecclesiastes 3:1–14.
27 See Isaiah 43:18–21.
28 See Acts 16:9–10.
29 For example, many of the social reforms in the UK during the nineteenth century were pioneered by those influenced by the evangelical revival of the previous years.
30 See Hebrews 2:4.
31 See 2 Timothy 3:16.
32 'Scripture, reason and tradition' have, for many years, been a helpful way of thinking theologically for those who are part of Anglicanism, the tradition into which I am ordained. It was John Wesley, the founder of the Methodists, who added 'experience'. That's why the four are known as the 'Wesleyan Quadrilateral'.
33 See 1 John 5:13; 1 Corinthians 15:13–20.
34 See Hebrews 9:27.
35 See John 3:16.

Notes

[36] See John 3:17–18; 2 Thessalonians 1:9; Jude 1:7; 2 Peter 2:4.

[37] See Romans 6:23.

O is for Obedience

[1] Paul Harcourt, *Growing in Circles* (East Malling: River Publishing/New Wine, 2016), p. 110.

[2] See 1 Samuel 15:22.

[3] See John 14:15.

[4] See 2 Corinthians 5:9.

[5] See Ephesians 6:1.

[6] See Ephesians 6:4.

[7] See Hebrews 13:17.

[8] See Luke 6:46.

[9] See Psalm 119:2; 2 John 1:6.

[10] See Luke 17:13.

[11] See Revelation 19:16.

[12] See Matthew 28:18.

[13] Acts 9:10.

[14] David Watson, *Discipleship* (London: Hodder & Stoughton, 1981, 1987), p. 24.

[15] See Mark 1:16–20; Luke 5:1–11.

[16] See John 21:15–19.

[17] See Luke 5:1–4.

[18] Luke 5:5.

[19] Malcolm Gladwell, *Outliers* (London: Penguin, 2009), ch. 2.

[20] See Ephesians 4:15.

[21] 1 Timothy 6:18.

[22] See Exodus 20:15.

[23] 1 Corinthians 6:18.

[24] Romans 12:21.

[25] See Exodus 20:13.

[26] Romans 12:13.

[27] Romans 13:6.
[28] See Matthew 7:24–27.
[29] Romans 12:2.
[30] See Romans 6:18.
[31] John 15:15.
[32] See Numbers 6:1–4; Luke 1:15.
[33] See, for example, Acts 18:18.
[34] See Matthew 19:12.
[35] See Matthew 7:11.
[36] Bill Johnson, *Manifesto for a Normal Christian Life* (London: The Elmbourne Press, 2012), p. 27.

P is for Prayer

[1] 'When you give' (Matthew 6:2).
[2] 'When you fast' (Matthew 6:16).
[3] 'When you pray' (Matthew 6:5).
[4] Luke 11:1.
[5] See Matthew 6:5–8; Isaiah 29:13.
[6] See Psalm 145:18.
[7] See 1 Peter 3:15.
[8] See 1 Timothy 2:8.
[9] See Psalm 95:6.
[10] See Daniel 10:12–14.
[11] See Luke 11:9–13.
[12] Nicky Gumbel, Twitter, 4 October 2013.
[13] See Ephesians 6:18–20.
[14] See Psalm 5:3; Mark 1:35.
[15] See Matthew 18:20.
[16] See Acts 1:14.
[17] Source unknown.
[18] See Galatians 5:16.
[19] 1 Thessalonians 5:17.

Q is for Quarrel

[1] An important exception should be made with matters relating to offences of public concern – particularly forms of abuse, including sexual abuse. Such matters are not just of personal concern between two individuals but are of public and civic importance and should be reported to civic authorities, who will act in accordance with established legal processes.

[2] Nicky Gumbel, Twitter, 21 September 2016.

[3] See 2 Corinthians 5:11–21.

[4] This is rarely adhered to today in much of the Western Church, perhaps for fear of misuse of power or accusations of intolerance.

[5] See Proverbs 3:28; Luke 8:17.

[6] See James 5:16; Proverbs 17:17.

[7] See 2 Corinthians 12:20.

[8] See Ephesians 4:27.

[9] See Ephesians 4:32.

[10] See James 1:19.

R is for Repentance

[1] See Mark 1:15; Acts 20:21.

[2] See Matthew 3:2; 4:17.

[3] See Luke 5:32.

[4] See Romans 2:4.

[5] See James 5:16.

[6] See Luke 15:11–32.

[7] See Genesis 6:6–7; 1 Samuel 15:11.

[8] See Romans 12:1–2.

[9] See John 15:1–8.

[10] See Matthew 3:8.

[11] See Genesis 12:1–5; Ezra 10; Acts 16:33–34.

[12] See Revelation 2:16.

[13] See Jonah 3:6–10.

[14] See Jeremiah 18:8; 2 Chronicles 7:14.

[15] See Acts 17:30: 2 Peter 3:9.

S is for Sacrament

[1] See Acts 8:38–39. Some churches, like The Belfrey, baptize infants of believing parents. When these children are ready to declare for themselves that they want to follow Christ for the rest of their lives, they take part in either Confirmation, or Affirmation of Baptismal Faith.

[2] See 2 Corinthians 5:17.

[3] Fred and Sharon Wright, *The World's Greatest Revivals* (Shippensburg, PA: Destiny Image, 2007), p. 255.

[4] At funerals, clergy sometimes say of a disciple that he/she has completed his/her baptism.

[5] With the exception of the thief in Luke 23:42–43, who trusted Christ as he was dying and so was not able to be baptized.

[6] See Acts 2:41; 10:47.

[7] See Colossians 2:12.

[8] See Romans 6:4.

[9] See Matthew 28:19.

[10] See Romans 10:9.

[11] See Luke 17:13.

[12] See 1 Timothy 6:15.

[13] See John 3:16.

[14] See Romans 5:8.

[15] See John 15:9–17.

[16] See Philippians 1:6.

[17] See Mark 16:16.

[18] Romans 6:11.

[19] See Matthew 26:26–29.

[20] See Acts 2:42; 20:7.

[21] See 1 Corinthians 11:33–34.

[22] See 1 Corinthians 11:28.

[23] See 1 Corinthians 11:26.

Notes

[24] See John 6:35, 53–58.

[25] So much so that John Wesley called it 'a converting ordinance'. (An ordinance is a religious rite.)

[26] See 1 Thessalonians 4:14.

T is for Trinity

[1] See Matthew 3:17.

[2] 1 Peter 1:2.

[3] 2 Corinthians 13:14.

[4] See John 14:16; 15:26; 16:14–15.

[5] See 1 John 4:8.

[6] See Matthew 6:21; Isaiah 29:13.

U is for Underprivileged

[1] See Psalm 12:5.

[2] See Exodus 23:6.

[3] See Deuteronomy 15:10–11.

[4] Psalm 41:1.

[5] See Luke 16:19–25.

[6] See Mathew 25:31–46.

[7] Galatians 2:10.

[8] John Grisham, speaking at Baptist Convention in 2008, cited in *Presbyterian Outlook*, 25 February 2008.

[9] We see this, for example, in the monastic movement of the early Middle Ages, the evangelical movement of the eighteenth century, the Oxford movement of the nineteenth century and the Pentecostal movement in the twentieth century.

[10] Bill Johnson, *Defining Moments* (New Kensington, PA: Whitaker House, 2016), p. 54.

[11] See Isaiah 61:1; Luke 4:18.

[12] See Galatians 6:10; 2 Thessalonians 3:13; and many examples in Titus, e.g. 3:1.

[13] See Acts 4:32–35.
[14] See Matthew 14:14.
[15] See Acts 10:4, 31.
[16] See Luke 7:18–22; Romans 14:17.

V is for Vision

[1] Bill Hybels, *Courageous Leadership* (Grand Rapids: Zondervan, 2002), p. 32.
[2] See Romans 4:16.
[3] See Genesis 12:1–9.
[4] See Acts 9:1–19.
[5] Mark 1:15.
[6] See Acts 13:4–7.
[7] Matthew 6:10.
[8] See Psalm 32:8.
[9] See Psalm 48:14.
[10] See Acts 20:22; John 16:13.
[11] Richard Branson, *Business Stripped Bare* (London: Virgin, 2008, 2009), p. 110.
[12] Joshua 24:15.
[13] Craig Groeschel, *If* (Grand Rapids: Zondervan, 2008), p. 60.
[14] See Habakkuk 2:2.
[15] See Isaiah 6:8.

W is for Worship

[1] See Malachi 1:8.
[2] Romans 12:1.
[3] See Hebrews 10:14.
[4] See Matthew 28:17.
[5] Matthew 2:11.
[6] See 1 Corinthians 12; Ephesians 5:18–20.

Notes

[7] See James 4:8.
[8] See Psalm 145:3.
[9] Tom Wright, *Simply Christian* (London: SPCK, 2006), p. 127.
[10] See Psalm 35:18.
[11] See Hebrews 10:25.
[12] See Psalms 33; 100.
[13] See Psalms 18:1; 116:1.
[14] See Psalm 92:1.
[15] See Colossians 3:16.
[16] See Ephesians 5:19.
[17] See Psalm 149:6.
[18] See Acts 16:25.
[19] See Psalm 73:17.
[20] See Psalm 126:3.
[21] See Psalm 34:3.
[22] See Psalms 42; 43; 137:1–6.
[23] Hebrews 13:15.
[24] See Psalms 103:13; 100:5.
[25] See Psalm 122:1.
[26] See Psalm 47:1.
[27] See Psalm 149:3.
[28] See Psalm 100:1.
[29] See Psalm 145:2.
[30] See Psalm 95:6.
[31] See Psalm 2:12.
[32] 1 Thessalonians 5:16–18.
[33] William Temple, *Christianity and the Social Order* (London: Macmillan, 1942), p. 17.
[34] David Watson, *Live a New Life* (Leicester: IVP, 1975), p. 33.

X is for X-rated

[1] See Genesis 2:17.
[2] Acts 15:29.

3   See Titus 2:12.
4   In the history of the church, leaders have occasionally told fol-
    lowers of Jesus to avoid certain things that, in retrospect, were
    not necessarily wrong. In writing this chapter I am aware I could
    be vulnerable to doing just this. To minimize that possibility, I've
    tried to limit this chapter to a few key areas that are clear in the
    Bible.
5   See 1 Corinthians 7:2; Exodus 22:16.
6   See Exodus 20:14.
7   See Romans 1:26–28; 1 Corinthians 6:9. This is now a profoundly
    counter-cultural perspective in twenty-first-century western
    society but is the consistent teaching of the Bible – the stand-
    ard by which followers of Jesus are called to live. This is not a
    homophobic perspective. There is no place for homophobia in the
    church or society, and all people should be treated with dignity,
    care and respect, irrespective of their sexuality or background.
8   See Galatians 5:21.
9   See Leviticus 18:23.
10 See 1 John 2:16.
11 See Hebrews 13:4.
12 See John 8:1–11; Luke 7:37–50.
13 See Matthew 5:9.
14 See Galatians 6:8.
15 See Proverbs 22:22; Amos 5:24; Matthew 6:22–23.
16 See Isaiah 1:15; Zechariah 7:8–10; Isaiah 61:7–8.
17 See Isaiah 61:1–3.
18 See Jeremiah 5:3–5, 26–31.
19 See Matthew 18:6.
20 See 1 Timothy 5:2; Galatians 3:28.
21 See Genesis 1:28–30.
22 See Psalm 24:1; Revelation 7:3.
23 See Galatians 5:21; Proverbs 20:1; Isaiah 5:11.
24 See Ephesians 5:18.
25 See Ephesians 4:29.
26 See James 3:5–6.
27 See Proverbs 20:19; James 4:11.

Notes

[28] See Ephesians 5:4.
[29] See Proverbs 17:27.
[30] See Proverbs 18:21; Psalm 19:14.
[31] See Luke 6:45.
[32] Philippians 4:8.

Y is for Yes!

[1] See 2 Corinthians 1:20.
[2] John 10:10.
[3] See Song of Songs 4.
[4] See Ephesians 4:15.
[5] See Ephesians 5:18.
[6] See Matthew 7:11.
[7] See Romans 8:31.
[8] See Numbers 6:24–26.
[9] See Psalm 27:1.
[10] See Exodus 15:26.
[11] See 1 Chronicles 17:19.
[12] See Joshua 23:14.
[13] See Psalm 145:13.
[14] See 2 Corinthians 7:1; 2 Peter 1:4.
[15] See Colossians 4:5–8; Matthew 5:16.
[16] See Galatians 1:10.
[17] See 1 Peter 1:15–16.
[18] See Psalm 119:148.
[19] See Acts 16:25.

Z is for Zeal

[1] See Ephesians 5:18.
[2] See 2 Timothy 4:7–8.

3   Romans 12:11.
4   See Hebrews 10:36.
5   See Psalm 42:5.
6   See James 1:12.
7   See Philippians 1:6.
8   See Hebrews 10:25.
9   See 1 Timothy 4:7–16.
10   See Colossians 3:17, 23–24.
11   See Psalm 69:9; Galatians 4:18.
12   2 Corinthians 8:22.
13   2 Corinthians 9:6.
14   See Joel 2:12; Revelation 3:19–20.
15   See, for example, Isaiah 9:7; 37:32.
16   See John 15:9.
17   See John 15:13.
18   Mark 12:30.
19   Genesis 1:31.
20   See Joshua 1:9; Proverbs 17:22–23; Psalm 27:1.
21   See Proverbs 29:25.
22   Brené Brown, *Rising Strong* (New York: Spiegel & Grau, 2015), p. 68.
23   See Matthew 6:25.
24   See Isaiah 41:10.
25   2 Timothy 1:7 (NET).
26   Revelation 22:17.

Index

Index

@bibleintro

*A Bible handbook for
the Twitter generation*

Chris Juby

A great introduction to the Bible, or a handy reference or
aide-mémoire for more in-depth study, *@bibleintro* offers a
succinct overview of the Bible.

Each book of the Bible is condensed to a tweet-length
summary, with:

\# A key people list
\# A key passage
\# Chapter summaries (as tweets)
\# A timeline illustrating where the book fits in to the overall
   story
\# A key insight based on the themes of the book

978-1-78078-124-2

God Conversations

Stories of how God speaks and what happens when we listen

Tania Harris

Stories of God talking to his people abound throughout the Bible, but we usually only get the highlights. We read: 'God said "Go to Egypt,"' and then, 'Mary and Joseph left for Egypt.' We're not told how God spoke, how they knew it was him, or how they decided to act on what they'd heard.

In *God Conversations*, international speaker and pastor Tania Harris shares insights from her own story of learning to hear God's voice. You'll get to eavesdrop on some contemporary conversations with God in the light of his communication with the ancients. Part memoir, part teaching, this unique and creative collection will help you to recognize God's voice when he speaks and what happens when you do.

978-1-78078-188-4

Authentic

We trust you enjoyed reading this book
from Authentic. If you want to be informed
of any new titles from this author and other
releases you can sign up to the Authentic
newsletter by contacting us:

By post:
Authentic Media Limited
PO Box 6326
Bletchley
Milton Keynes
MK1 9GG

E-mail:
info@authenticmedia.co.uk

Follow us: